# SILCHESTER REVEALED

## The Iron Age and Roman Town of Calleva

*For*

*Stephen and Caroline Butt*

*and*

*The Calleva Foundation*

# SILCHESTER REVEALED

## *The Iron Age and Roman Town of Calleva*

Michael Fulford

WIND*gather*
PRESS

Windgather Press is an imprint of Oxbow Books

Published in the United Kingdom in 2021 by
OXBOW BOOKS
The Old Music Hall, 106–108 Cowley Road, Oxford, OX4 1JE

and in the United States by
OXBOW BOOKS
1950 Lawrence Road, Havertown, PA 19083

Paperback Edition: ISBN 978-1-911188-83-4
Digital Edition: ISBN 978-1-911188-84-1 (epub)

A CIP record for this book is available from the British Library

Printed in the United Kingdom by Short Run Press

For a complete list of Windgather titles, please contact:

United Kingdom
OXBOW BOOKS
Telephone (01865) 241249
Fax (01865) 794449
Email: oxbow@oxbowbooks.com
www.oxbowbooks.com

United States of America
OXBOW BOOKS
Telephone (610) 853-9131
Fax (610) 853-9146
Email: queries@casemateacademic.com
www.casemateacademic.com/oxbow

Oxbow Books is part of the Casemate group

Front cover: View across Calleva from the north-west, © Dae Sasitorn
Back cover: Reconstructed view of the town as it might have appeared in the later
3rd century, © Historic England Archive

Text layout by Frabjous Books

# Contents

# List of figures

# Acknowledgements

........................................................................................................................

The possibility of writing this book owes a great deal to very many people, not least the thousands of students and volunteers who, over the years, have carried out the hard and painstaking task of excavating the sites from which all our new knowledge of Silchester stems. But none of this would have happened but for the continuing support of my wife, Charlotte, and my family, and my University, the University of Reading, which appointed me lecturer in archaeology in 1974, the same year when I was first invited to undertake an excavation at Silchester. Right from the beginning, the University has expected grants to be found to support fieldwork, even when it forms a core part of the curriculum, and a great many public and private organisations, as well as private individuals have awarded grants and made donations in support of our work at Silchester. While, historically, these have all been appropriately acknowledged and thanked in connection with their support of individual projects, I wish to single out certain individuals who have made really significant contributions which have ensured the continuity of projects at challenging times: first and foremost, the generosity of Stephen and Caroline Butt and the Calleva Foundation, which has stimulated exciting new research at Silchester, particularly on its Iron Age origins, while at the same time ensuring a lasting legacy through publication of the results of the fieldwork, has been absolutely exceptional. By galvanising a small group of supporters, Dudley Fishburn has played an invaluable role in ensuring the continuity of fieldwork, notably by helping to rescue the huge Insula IX excavation from premature closure in the early 2000s.

Archaeology is all about teamwork and the successful accomplishment of the Insula IX excavation and those that have followed since owes a huge amount to my colleague and co-director, Amanda Clarke. Simply put, without Amanda, none of the work which has taken place since 1997 would have happened. More recently I have been fortunate to have had the support of Jen Eaton, Nick Pankhurst and Dan Wheeler, who have been crucial to the successful completion of projects in and out of the field. I am also very grateful to them, and to Rob Fry and Sarah Lambert-Gates, for the critical role they have played in illustrating this book. I also wish to thank Nina Crummy for all her help and advice in the preparation of this book. Finally, I return to Silchester to thank the owner of the Roman town, Hampshire County Council, for giving me permission to carry out excavations within the town, to Silchester villagers, and to Biddy and Nick West who, ever since their purchase of The Old Manor House in 1979, have been a constant source of support, year after year, to me and all the students and volunteers who have taken part in the excavations.

# Preface

This book is a response to the frequent requests I have received over recent years for a new account of Silchester. My excuse up to now is that I am still in the middle of projects, but, in fact, there is already an enormous of new material to bring together and make more accessible to a wider public, and there is no excuse for not getting on with this now!

Silchester is a special place for me as it is to many. Standing on the bank behind the massive Roman city wall where it survives high above the South Gate gives one an immediate appreciation of the scale and setting of Iron Age and Roman Silchester. The view to the south stretches over field and woodland as far as the Hampshire Downs, emphasising the commanding position of the settlement over the surrounding countryside. Turning to look north, one has an uninterrupted view right across the city to the North Gate almost exactly a kilometre away. From the South Gate, the line of the city wall can be followed almost all the way around to give a vivid sense of the space occupied by one of the major cities of Iron Age and Roman Britain; 107 acres (c 43.3 hectares) altogether, smaller than the area of an average English village. The imagination can begin to fill the now empty space within the walls with buildings, perhaps of the Roman city in its heyday in the 2nd century, perhaps of the Iron Age town founded almost 200 years earlier, or of the city in its slow decline after AD 400. And right above you the skylark sings in summer!

Silchester has been a subject of interest and speculation since the time of Leland and Camden, over 400 years ago, but only from the 1860s has there been any systematic attempt to explore the remains within the walls. The work of those early excavators was brought expertly together by George Boon in his classic, richly informed survey, *Silchester: the Roman Town of Calleva*. This was published almost 50 years ago in 1974, the same year I conducted my first excavation at Silchester on the defences close to the South Gate. In the same way that Boon's *Silchester* brought together previous discoveries, especially the results of the Society of Antiquaries of London's 20-year campaign (1890–1909) to excavate the entirety of the Roman city and some of its external earthworks, this time of Covid-19 and the cancellation of fieldwork in 2020 has given me an opportunity to pull together and reflect on the achievements of the last 46 years of research. Just as the results of each year's work by the Antiquaries were published annually in the Society's specialist journal, *Archaeologia*, much of the work since 1974 has been published at length in academic monographs and journals. Any ambition to synthesise the achievements of the Antiquaries at the conclusion of their excavations and disseminate them to a wider audience was lost with the outbreak of World War I and had to wait almost half a century for Boon's original synthesis, *Roman Silchester*, published in 1957. Happily, this synthesis has been put together before my excavations and their publication are even complete.

Although my own work at Silchester is not yet finished, a great deal has been done and it is time to try and bring together and reflect on the results of what has been achieved so far. Whereas the antiquarian work of the early 20th century was extensive but only – and literally – superficial, revealing insula by insula, plan by plan, the great majority of the masonry-founded buildings within the city walls, the advances of archaeological methodologies through the 20th century were such that vast amounts of information can be derived from much smaller interventions. But, just as methodologies have advanced, so have their associated costs. As we shall see in Chapter 1, the complete excavation and publication of just one block of the city would require an almost unimaginable scale of resources today.

Given the much more limited spatial extent of the excavations undertaken since 1974, what has been achieved? Most important, perhaps, has been the realisation that the Roman city and whatever lies beneath is very well preserved. Contrary to the belief that little remained to be discovered after the conclusion of excavation within the city in 1908, a view reinforced by the disappointing results of the re-excavation of the church in 1961, a small trial investigation in 1977 in the forum basilica, the great public building in the heart of the city, led to a project (1980–1986) which revealed a sequence of early Roman buildings and, deeper still, the Iron Age occupation, all well preserved beneath it. The major excavation which followed in Insula IX (1997–2014) provided further confirmation that both the Roman and the underlying Iron Age archaeology were well preserved despite the Society of Antiquaries' earlier work. Extrapolation from these two excavations, reinforced by subsequent investigations within the city, suggests that at least 80% of the archaeology preserved at the outset of the Society of Antiquaries' excavations in 1890 remains undisturbed to this day.

Between them, those two major excavations within the city, conducted over a period of more than 30 years, have given remarkable insight into its Iron Age origins and the character of the settlement and its inhabitants in those formative years of the settlement. At the same time, thanks to the advances that have been made in the study of both material culture and environmental evidence, we have been able to build up a picture of the changing life of the city and its inhabitants, gaining knowledge of their living conditions, diet, health, occupations, leisure activities, ritual behaviour and so on, over more than 400 years.

Research continues and it is hoped that, like George Boon, whose first *Roman Silchester* was published in 1957, it will be possible to follow this book with a subsequent edition which draws on the current and very recently completed programmes of excavations.

So, since 1974 we can now add a whole new phase, Iron Age Calleva, to the story of Silchester, and to the Roman city we can now bring time-depth and the beginnings of a fleshing-out of the lives of successive generations of its inhabitants.

Michael Fulford
University of Reading
December 2020

# CHAPTER ONE

# Discovering Calleva

The most significant development in the history of investigations into the Iron Age and Roman town at Silchester was the great, 20-year long, project by the Society of Antiquaries of London to reveal what, at the time, was thought to be the complete plan of the town within its defensive walls. The excavations took place between 1890 and 1909, providing the first glimpse of the entirety of a Roman town in Britain and indeed of any town within the Roman world, even celebrated Pompeii. The town was confirmed to have been divided into regular insulae (Latin = islands), the great majority containing a number of buildings ranging from well-decorated private houses to modest shop or workshop premises, a few also with a temple or possible temple, one with a possible church, and the whole protected by the massive town wall. A few blocks were dominated by the public buildings they contained: the great forum basilica at the centre, dominating the town; the public baths at the lowest point of the town by the springs in the south-east quarter; the trio of temples in their enclosure by the east gate; and the inn with its attached bath house by the South Gate. The influence of the main thoroughfare, the east–west street which carried traffic between London and the west of Britain, can easily be seen in the crowding together, side-by-side, of narrow-fronted shops-cum-workshops competing for business along its length (Figs 1.1–2).

As we will see, there is a background of cumulative discoveries to this revelatory work, but it was a combination of factors which determined that Silchester was the first Roman town to be explored in this way. First and foremost it was a greenfield site only impinged upon by the parish church of St Mary the Virgin and the farm and farm buildings on its eastern side, but it was also in the single ownership of a sympathetic landowner, the

Duke of Wellington, and the influential antiquarian society, the Society of Antiquaries of London, was keen to sponsor excavation. With large open areas within their walls, other Roman town sites offered similar potential: Aldborough of the Brigantes in Yorkshire, Caistor St Edmunds of the Iceni in Norfolk, Verulamium of the Catuvellauni beside St Albans in Hertfordshire and Wroxeter of the Cornovii, in Shropshire (Fig. 1.3). Across the River Severn in south-east Wales was the site of Caerwent, the chief town of the Silures, which, though the Roman town was partly buried beneath the village which had developed over it, followed Silchester to be the second most explored town of Roman Britain. Most of the other greenfield Roman towns saw substantial area excavations in the first half of the 20th century, but with none revealing more than parts of their whole town plan. Despite its shortcomings, as we shall see, the 'complete' plan of Roman Silchester has been published repeatedly through the 20th and into the present century and, as a consequence, arguably still remains the best-known Roman town in Britain. The background to the decision in 1890 to excavate Silchester can now be explored.

Despite being shrouded in trees and vegetation, the impressive remains

FIGURE 1.1 Aerial view of Silchester taken in 1976 looking towards the east, showing part of the Iron Age defences, the Roman street grid and outlines of some of the buildings (courtesy Chris Stanley)

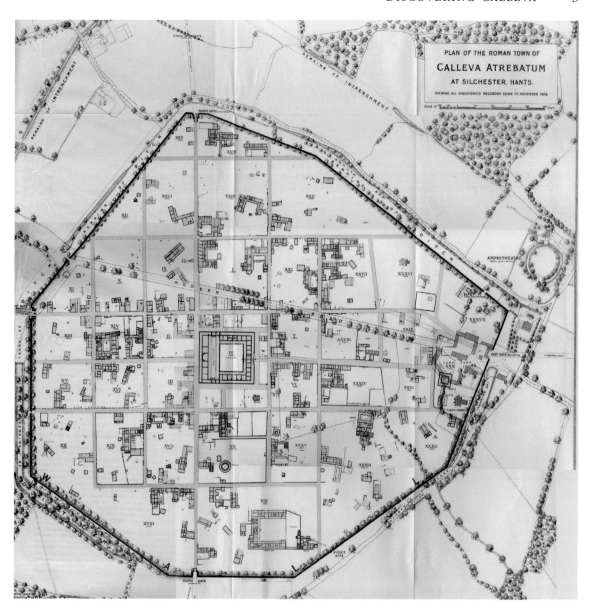

PLAN OF THE ROMAN TOWN OF
**CALLEVA ATREBATUM**
AT SILCHESTER, HANTS.
SHEWING ALL DISCOVERIES RECORDED DOWN TO NOVEMBER 1908.

FIGURE 1.2 The plan of Calleva after the completion of excavations by the Society of Antiquaries within the town walls in 1908

of its circuit of town walls, a mile and a half in length and enclosing a little over 100 acres (40+ hectares), had attracted antiquarians' interest in Silchester since the 16th century. Among them was William Stukeley who visited Silchester in 1724 and, while recognising the amphitheatre for what it is, mistakenly depicted the town in the form of a rectangular military fort with its characteristic 'playing card' plan (Fig. 1.4). Although the outline of streets, which became visible each summer as the crop ripened, had been

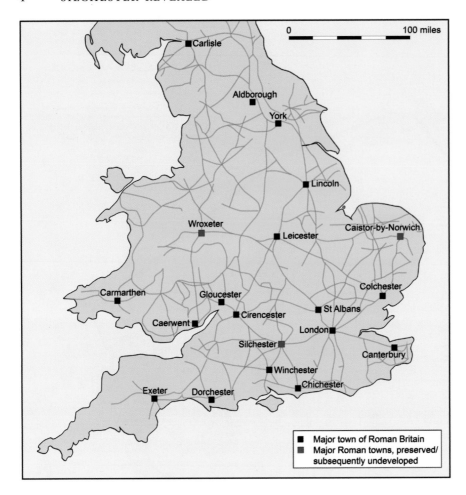

FIGURE 1.3 Map of Britain showing the locations of the major Roman towns

commented on by Camden in his great survey, *Britannia*, first published in English in 1610, it was the surveyor John Wright who was the first to attempt a systematic record of these and the town walls in 1745 (Fig. 1.5).

Various accounts record digging taking place within the walls in the 18th and 19th centuries but with little information as to what was found. It was not until 1864 that excavations took place which were of a more scientific character, being recorded in some detail and eventually published in summary form. This was the work of the Reverend James Joyce, the rector of Stratfield Saye, who was encouraged by the second Duke of Wellington to undertake excavations, the manor of Silchester having been acquired by the first Duke in 1828. Joyce left two beautifully illustrated bound notebooks and a sketchbook, now in Reading Museum, full of information about the individual buildings and structures that his workmen had uncovered as well

FIGURE 1.4 William
Stukeley's illustration
of the amphitheatre in
1724

The Side view of the Amphitheater at Silchester.   May 8. 1724.

FIGURE 1.5 John Wright's
plan of the town in 1745

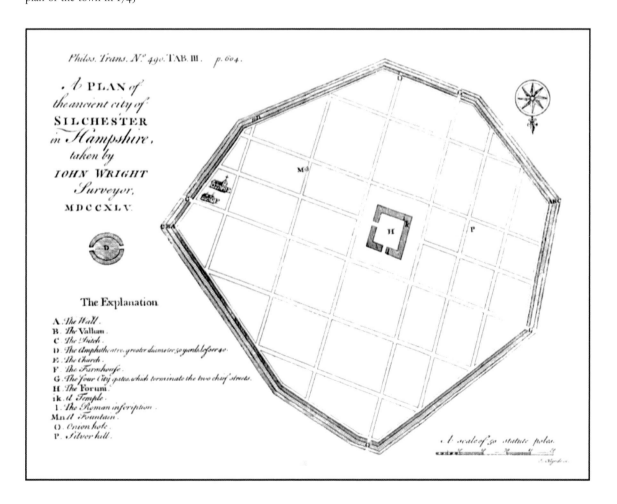

as about his methods of excavation (Fig. 1.6). While his work mainly laid bare the ground plans of the structures he found, it is clear that he also appreciated the importance of stratigraphy and how that could help him understand change over time and how to date buildings from independently dated objects, such as coins, associated with them. We see this, for example, in his interpretation of one of his most important discoveries, the forum basilica, the central building of the Roman town, which is understood to have accommodated administrative and judicial functions. Although Joyce and his team of four workmen excavated in several parts of the town within the walls, it is his work on the town gates, the forum basilica, the houses in Insula I and XXIII and the temple in Insula VII which are the most important, not least because they were published. His outstanding single find is undoubtedly the fine bronze 'Silchester' eagle which, along with other objects, was displayed in Stratfield Saye House, home of the Duke

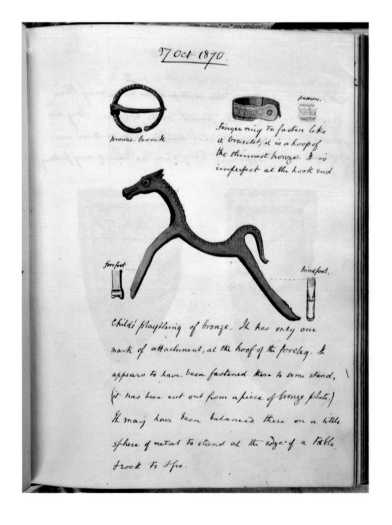

FIGURE 1.6  Page dated 17 October 1870 from Joyce's diary illustrating the fine copper alloy mount or handle known as the 'Silchester horse'

FIGURE 1.7 The Silchester Eagle discovered by Joyce's workmen in 1866. Made in bronze, it probably dates from the 1st century AD. It may have formed part of a statue of Jupiter or an imperial person, the eagle at the foot of the figure looking up

of Wellington (Figs 1.7, 3.18). These included a complete mosaic floor and fragments of two others which were lifted and re-laid in the entrance hall (Figs 1.8, 7.5). Excavation continued in a desultory way after his death, aged only 59, in 1878, including with the discovery of the large building and bath house near the South Gate which is very probably the mansio of the town. This was the accommodation reserved for officials and other users of the imperial posting service (cursus publicus).

FIGURE 1.8 Second century mosaic from Insula I, House 1 discovered in 1864 and re-laid in the front hall of Stratfield Saye House

# Uncovering the town

It was Joyce's work which drew the attention of General Pitt Rivers, the first Government Inspector of Ancient Monuments, and the Society of Antiquaries of London to the remains at Silchester and the potential they had for revealing, for the first time, a complete plan of a Roman town. With the agreement of the third Duke of Wellington, a project began in 1890 sponsored by the Society of Antiquaries which was to last 20 years and was to reveal what was thought at the time to be the complete plan of the town within the walls. The excavation was directed by W. H. St John Hope, a senior official of the Society, and George E. Fox, an artist-architect and student of Roman Britain. Wherever possible the area was dug insula by insula with individual buildings identified by parallel narrow trenches dug systematically and diagonally across each one (Fig. 1.9). The insulae were individually numbered, the total amounting to 37 (Fig. 1.2). As wall foundations were discovered, they were followed to define the individual buildings which were then excavated to floor level (Fig. 1.10). The trenches were sounded for soft spots which might conceal the tops of pits or wells, which, on excavation, often turned out to contain well preserved artefacts, including items of organic materials such as the wooden barrels used to line the wells (Fig. 1.11), and two great hoards of ironwork, as well as very many examples of complete pots. There was methodological innovation, too, most notably by the geologist, Clement Reid, who, with his assistant,

FIGURE 1.9
Antiquarian excavation techniques: Left: plan of trenching across the north-east of Insula IX in 1893; right: geophysics detects traces of the Society of Antiquaries' trial trenching across the whole town 1890–1908 (adapted from Creighton with Fry 2016, fig. 3.8)

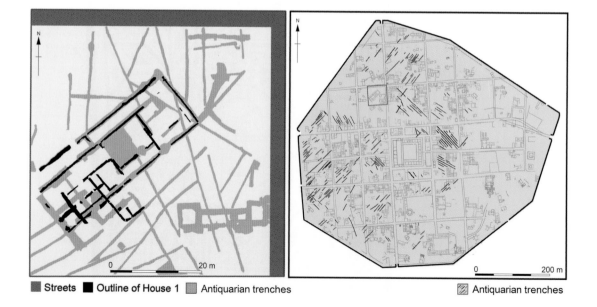

Streets    Outline of House 1    Antiquarian trenches            Antiquarian trenches

FIGURE I.10 The temple in Insula XXXV excavated by the Society of Antiquaries in 1907. The spoil heaps from Joyce's excavation of the forum basilica can be seen in the background

FIGURE I.11 Imported wine-barrels of silver fir, subsequently re-used to line wells. Note the workmen and the scale.

A. H. Lyell, recovered waterlogged seeds and insects from pits and wells each year from 1899 onwards. Reid identified a range of horticultural crops introduced by the Romans and grown in Britain, as well as traded items from the Mediterranean such as figs and grapes or raisins, though the latter could eventually have been grown locally.

FIGURE 1.12 Inscription carved in Purbeck Marble found in 1907 associated with the temple in Insula XXXV. It records a dedication which provides confirmation that Calleva was the ancient name of Silchester: CALLEVAE can be read in the penultimate line from the bottom

The year's work was reported in the Society's journal *Archaeologia* and included both overall plans of each insula and more detailed plans and descriptions of individual buildings and a summary of the more notable finds. Excavation within the walls was completed in 1908 and a final season of work took place the following year on the outlying earthworks and some Roman pottery kilns accidentally discovered to the north of the town. No excavation was undertaken on the amphitheatre and no attempt was made to locate extramural cemeteries. Over the years there had been much speculation as to the Roman name of the town, but this was brought to an end by the discovery in 1907 in a temple in Insula XXXV of an inscription carved on Purbeck marble recording a dedication by a guild (collegium) of foreigners (peregrini) confirming that the town was indeed Calleva, an identification first mooted in the early 18th century (Fig. 1.12).

FIGURE 1.13 Excavators' rubbish: mineral water 'Codd' bottles of Allen and Sons of Basingstoke, and of Basingstoke and Aldershot; and of C. Marchant of Reading, a tea cup and whisky bottle disposed of by the excavators of Insula IX, probably in 1893, and re-discovered in 1997

The excavations recovered a large number of finds, but by no means all were kept, particularly those of animal bone, building materials, whether of stone or brick, and pottery sherds, all of which were found in very large numbers (Fig. 1.13). Attention focused on rare finds, such as of sculptured fragments or inscriptions, and on metalwork, mostly of copper alloy, including coins, which are the most numerous find in this metal, but also well preserved ironwork.

Complete or exceptional pieces of pottery, such as decorated sherds of the fine, imported red table ware known as samian, were also kept as were complete examples of the different types of building materials, such as roof tiles or the flue tiles used to conduct the hot air up the walls of heated rooms. The more interesting and better preserved mosaics were also lifted for display in Reading Museum. On the initiative of the founder and honorary curator of Reading Museum, Joseph Stevens, the great collection was first received on loan from the Duke of Wellington and then purchased from the Estate in 1978. The Silchester Gallery remains a highlight of the museum's collection. Perhaps surprising, in the aftermath of the project, was the lack of any overview of the results for wider public consumption. It took almost half a century before George Boon, then assistant in Reading Museum, published his synthesis *Roman Silchester: the archaeology of a Romano-British town* in 1957, subsequently revised as *Silchester: the Roman Town of Calleva* (1974). That this has remained the standard work of reference on the town for almost 50 years is a tribute to its fine quality.

The recovery of the plan of the Roman town and its constituent buildings was unquestionably a major achievement but it left many questions. First, the methodology of trial trenching was only capable of locating buildings with masonry foundations and the plan revealed many apparently empty spaces across the town. Were these really devoid of structures, or did they contain timber buildings? In what other ways might those spaces have been used? For example, for gardens, or for orchards, or, perhaps, for grazing? Second, in concentrating on clearing only to the floor level of each building as it was discovered, no attempt was made to build on the stratigraphic observations made by Joyce and to try and recover evidence with which to date the buildings or to disentangle the underlying build up of occupation which we now know averages about a metre in depth across the town. We are left then with a collection of undated buildings and of finds, the latter for the most part without provenance, all of which amount to a town without a history. Although Iron Age coins carrying the legend CALLEV or CALLE were known of by the late 19th century and there was awareness of the possibility of finding Iron Age remains, the excavators admitted in their final report that they had found nothing to advance knowledge of possible pre-Roman occupation (Fig. 1.14).

Although excavations since 1909 have now

FIGURE 1.14 Iron Age gold quarter stater of Eppillus marked CALLEV (courtesy, the late George Boon)

0        5 mm

contributed to our knowledge of the chronology of several buildings, the great majority still remain undated. However, from the information gained from excavations in other towns in southern Britain, we observe that it is rare to find buildings (other than bath houses and some public buildings) with masonry foundations before the second half of the 2nd century. Consequently, it is probably safe to generalise and observe that the plan that we have is that of the town of the mid-to-late Roman period. Allowing that we now also know that the town walls were built in the late 3rd century we can propose that, albeit lacking any indication of the existence or prevalence of timber buildings, the Society of Antiquaries' great excavation project has given us a plan of the town around AD 300 (or in the range 250–350).

## New techniques

If we consider that the lack of chronology was the most significant deficiency of the Antiquaries' excavations, it was the first where steps were taken to address it. Between the two World Wars Mortimer Wheeler led the way in developing the methodology of excavating stratigraphically and of recording the resulting sequence of occupation. Stratigraphic excavation involves the peeling away of layers of soil, each distinguished from the next by differences in colour and texture, from the most recent down to the earliest, all the while ensuring that the finds from each layer are kept together as a collection for subsequent study to establish its character and date of deposition. This approach was first applied at Silchester by Mrs Aylwin Cotton, who had trained under Wheeler and then undertook excavations for the Office of Works in 1938–9 on the rampart behind the town wall, as well as on the upstanding earthworks, presumed to be of prehistoric date, to the west of the town walls. By excavating sections through it down to the gravel, the natural geology, beneath, she showed that the rampart was constructed in 160–170 and that the town wall itself, which was already known to be a later replacement, was added about 190–210 (though subsequent work in the 1960s and '70s has revised this date downwards to around 280). Obtaining dating evidence for the outer earthworks, employing the same approach of excavating a section through the bank and accompanying ditch down to the underlying natural gravels, was less successful. The section through the north-western, Sawyer's Land rampart, produced no useful evidence, while the trench into the tail of the bank in Rampier's Copse produced mid-1st century AD pottery, though the original building of the bank was probably much earlier.

The period between the two World Wars also saw the establishment of a new technique of archaeological prospection – aerial photography. Whether through the parching of the grass or the ripening of cereals through lack of moisture, revealing the outlines of shallowly buried streets and buried buildings, or through the opposite, the sustained relative greening of grass or crops where they overlay ditches retaining moisture, new sites of all periods were discovered across the British Isles. For Silchester aerial photography revealed a previously undiscovered defence of the town, part of which could be seen to run beneath streets and the town walls and, by implication, must therefore be early in date. Excavation by George Boon in the 1950s of sections across the line of this feature both within and without the town walls did indeed demonstrate the existence of a substantial defensive ditch, some 13.5 m wide and 3.5 m deep, which enclosed about 38 hectares (83 acres), an area about four-fifths the size of what became the walled Roman town. As well as verifying that what had been observed from the air was indeed a major archaeological feature, the excavation of what Boon called 'The Inner Earthwork' provided evidence of date, placing it in the period AD 25–50, the years leading up to and around the Roman Conquest of south-east Britain.

Following the last season of excavation within the town walls by the Society of Antiquaries in 1908, no excavation was to be undertaken to re-examine any of the intramural buildings for over 50 years. This changed in 1961 with the decision by Professor Sir Ian Richmond to re-excavate the building which the original excavator, William St John Hope, had claimed, but without indisputable proof, in 1892 to be a Christian church (Fig. 1.15).

FIGURE 1.15
The Silchester 'church' undergoing re-excavation by Sir Ian Richmond in 1961; view to the west

What might Richmond have expected of fresh excavation? A date, certainly and also some confirmatory evidence, such as artefacts of clearly Christian character, that the building was indeed a church. Further, there was also the hope of discovering beneath it a yet earlier house church – a private house used as a church. The results were disappointing: no Christian artefacts were found and, though datable pottery was found beneath the floor, it only indicated the building was later than 200. All that remained was the ground plan which, after careful analysis and comparison with early churches elsewhere in the empire, was argued in the full publication of the results in 1976 to be indeed that of a Christian church. Disappointing, too, was the lack of evidence for an earlier, underlying building. On the positive side and of enduring value, however, and reflecting the advances in techniques of excavation and recording as advocated by Wheeler were the detailed plans, photographs and description of the remains, representing a very significant development on the brief account of 1892.

The later 20th century saw major advances in many areas of archaeology: prospection, techniques of excavation, and the systematic analysis of material culture and of environmental evidence including quantitative approaches to the data. Instead of remarking on the presence of particular types of artefact, animal bone or seed or plant remain, as was the case at the start of the century, it became routine to assess their importance relative to one another and, thanks to the advances in our ability to excavate and interpret the complex stratigraphy of an urban site like Silchester, determine how their representation changed over time. Whereas the early excavators had been extremely selective in what they retained at the end of the season, now it became essential to keep more-or-less everything for subsequent research. In the case of bulky, space-consuming finds like building material that work had to be done on site with disposal taking place during the excavation. Sub-disciplines such as archaeobotany, zooarchaeology and the study of pottery changed beyond all recognition. Out of this has developed important new knowledge, for example of the types of plants grown, imported and consumed; of the varying preferences for different types of meat and fish; and of the changing trade networks evidenced in the supply of pottery, among the most abundant and durable artefacts to survive in the archaeological record, from different parts of Britain and the wider Roman world.

Essential to the development of the growing number of specialist research topics was the need for systematic recovery: it was not possible to recover microscopic seeds and plant remains, nor the bones of small mammals, birds or fish, nor indeed tiny artefacts like glass beads or the microscopic waste from iron forging through hand excavation. Flotation tanks became a routine part of excavation equipment. Pumps enabled water to be passed through representative bulk samples of the soil from individual layers, especially from rubbish pits and wells, in order to float off carbonised remains like charcoal, seeds and other plant remains (Fig. 1.16). This left the residues to be carefully sorted for the artefacts and ecofacts typically otherwise missed by hand excavation. These approaches are time and labour consuming and depend on strict sampling regimes to ensure they are representative. Before this technique was developed, the only seeds, wood or plant remains discovered had been carbonised by burning, but now they could be found, along with insect remains, by the methodical analysis of

FIGURE 1.16 Flotation in action at Silchester 2015: Rory Williams Burrell

samples from waterlogged deposits. Latrine deposits, where human waste generates high concentrations of phosphates and calcium, provide a medium for the preservation by mineralisation of food remains which have been eaten, thus providing direct insight into diet.

Other techniques introduced into excavation strategies and employed at Silchester from the late 1990s include micromorphology: the taking of blocks of soil from stratigraphic sequences, such as the occupation sequence within a building, to understand better its composition and characterise change over time in a way virtually impossible to achieve through hand excavation (Fig. 1.17). A slice, ground and polished down to a thickness of 30 microns, taken from a block of soil set hard in resin can be immensely revealing about the nature of the occupation. Examples include the discovery of microscopic evidence of animal dung indicating a building's use as a stable and of the way floors were surfaced, including the use of mats on the earthen floor of a domestic dwelling. The elemental composition of the soil can also be revealing about the nature of the occupation, for example high concentrations of metals such as copper or lead compared with the background levels from the local geology, are likely to be indicative of metalworking. Previously, the identification of this activity had been reliant on the discovery of larger masses of waste slag or of crucibles or moulds which could readily be recognised and recovered by hand excavation. However, if such remains had been regularly cleaned out of a workshop there would be no clue, other than the concentrations of metals in the soil, as to the nature of the activities which had taken place within it. Another example is afforded by phosphorus, where high levels attributable to animal dung may indicate the presence of domestic animals.

Considering the masses of artefacts and organic material recovered from an excavation such as at Silchester, a whole battery of new techniques of more forensic analysis has been developed in the last 20–30 years and begun to be applied both to single items and, on a larger scale, to collections of material, including those from Silchester. By studying the composition of artefacts it is possible to gain insights into the materials used and the development of technologies of manufacture as well as of their provenance. The application of geological techniques of provenancing, where slices of the material, reduced to a thickness of only 30 microns, can be analysed under the microscope, has been applied with great effect to artefacts of stone and fired clay. For example, it has been possible to determine that the black, white, red and yellow stone tesserae (small cubes) used in the making of the first mosaics laid in houses and bath buildings in Silchester and elsewhere

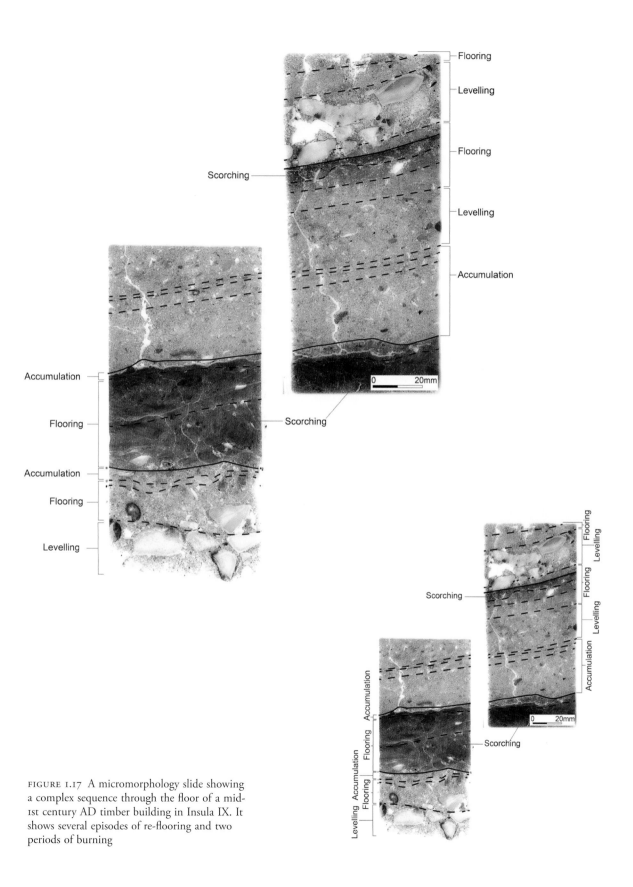

FIGURE 1.17 A micromorphology slide showing a complex sequence through the floor of a mid-1st century AD timber building in Insula IX. It shows several episodes of re-flooring and two periods of burning

FIGURE 1.18 A fragment of mosaic from the public baths. The individual tesserae are of a distinctive, hard chalk which was quarried from near Corfe on the Isle of Purbeck, south-east Dorset

in southern Britain originated from the Isle of Purbeck in south-east Dorset (Fig. 1.18). In the case of pottery, one example, where analysis has shown a distant provenance, is a distinctive type of late Iron Age pottery where the inclusions in the clay correspond with rock types found in the Auvergne region of Central France.

A remarkable recent development has been that of using gas chromatography and gas chromatography-mass spectometry to extract and identify the residues left from food preparation on the internal surfaces of cooking pots. The analysis of a group of late Iron Age pots from Silchester has shown that they were used to process animal meat and fat, mostly of ruminants like cattle and sheep, but also of pig, along with some plant products. Surprisingly, though milk was found to be characteristic of the residues of pots of earlier Iron Age communities in the region, no evidence was found of it or other dairy products at Silchester in the late Iron Age.

FIGURE 1.19 Insula IX: miniature dog buried in the foundation trench of the late Iron Age hall. Its oxygen and strontium isotopes indicate an origin in France or south-west Germany

Techniques used to analyse stable isotopes of carbon and nitrogen preserved in human and animal remains have provided valuable insight into diet, while the analysis of the stable isotopes of strontium and oxygen have been helpful in providing insights into where people and animals were first raised. The strontium isotope can be linked by diet to the local geology, while the oxygen isotope can be linked to rainwater whose composition is influenced by geographical and climatic factors. In the case of Silchester these kinds of analysis, using teeth from two, very rare, miniature 'lapdogs', one of late Iron Age, the other of earliest Roman date, demonstrated that the earlier of the two almost certainly originated from outside of Britain, perhaps from France or further east in south-west Germany (Fig. 1.19). That the earlier dog was special with a high status association is indicated by its burial in the foundations of the great late Iron Age hall discovered beneath the Roman occupation excavated in Insula IX, to be returned to below and in Chapter Two.

Just as modern methodologies of excavation and recording can produce far more information compared with the earlier and mid-20th century, so, too, the development of scientific techniques has shown how much can be extracted from single or small groups of artefacts or biological material. Together they permit the possibility of obtaining a rich characterisation of life within the town addressing questions about the nature of the built environment and the use of space, and the identity, diet and occupations of the inhabitants and how all these changed over time between the late Iron Age and the abandonment of the town between the 5th and the 7th centuries AD. However, considering that an urban excavation of any scale is likely to produce records of thousands of different layers with each potentially containing large numbers of finds of different types, it is impossible to make sense of all of this without a computerised database which permits integration of the different strands of information and allows them to be organised, phase by phase, building by building and so on. Since 1997 Silchester has been fortunate in having access to just such a database, the Integrated Archaeological Database (IADB).

## What next?

Given the enormous potential of all these developments, we need to ask how they have impacted on and been exploited by recent and ongoing investigations of Silchester's archaeology? First, growing confidence in our ability as archaeologists to explore complex, stratified archaeology encouraged a step change in our approach to excavation through the investigation of the stratigraphy which was either sealed beneath the buildings revealed and planned by Joyce and the Society of Antiquaries or, among the 'empty' spaces, apparently not explored except by narrow trial trenches. Although the results from the re-excavation of the church in 1961 had not been encouraging in that no underlying structures were discovered, work on re-excavating the South and North Gates of the town, respectively in 1975 and 1991, showed that there was much to be gained by new work, just by exposing again at what had been found in the 19th and early 20th centuries. With these two main gates it could be shown that they may have originally stood alone as monumental markers of the boundaries of the town and then, about AD 200, they were incorporated into the mid-Roman defence consisting of an earthen rampart and ditch encircling the town (Chapter 6). What is certain is that they were standing when the town wall was built up against them. We also found in 1976 that the narrow south-east gate had been designed as a postern to link the inn (mansio) with a building detected by aerial photography just outside the walls. It was not a sluice gate to control the flow of water out of the town as the Antiquaries' had thought. These results were promising and encouraged a return to investigating the interior of the town to see what might survive of the presumed late Iron Age and early Roman occupation which pre-dated the custom of building the kind of foundations in masonry which the early excavators had recognised as they worked their way across the town.

The monumental forum basilica seemed to offer potential for investigation (Chapters 3–5). It was by some measure the largest building in the town and it appeared to have been built out on a terrace with the ground stepping down beyond it to the south. Only excavation could test the hypothesis that it sealed and preserved any underlying occupation which might have preceded its construction. This did indeed prove to be the case and over seven seasons of excavation, 1980–1986, the late Iron Age occupation was revealed at the base of the almost metre deep stratigraphic sequence contained within the massive foundations of the great hall (basilica) on the west side of the complex. Above that were stratified the remains of two previously unknown major Roman buildings constructed of timber and

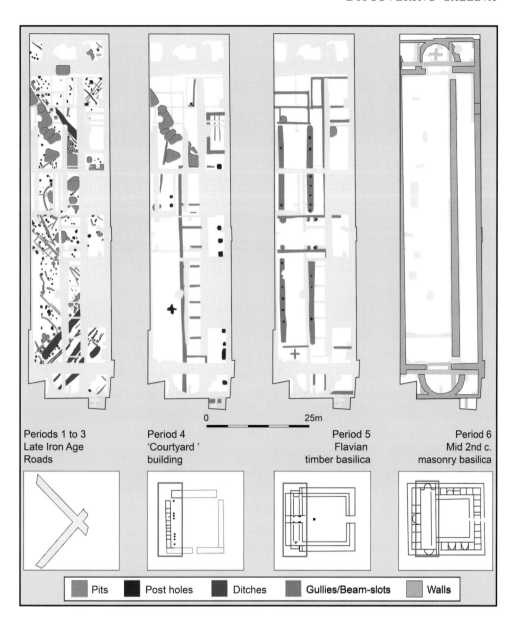

Periods 1 to 3
Late Iron Age
Roads

Period 4
'Courtyard'
building

Period 5
Flavian
timber basilica

Period 6
Mid 2nd c.
masonry basilica

0        25m

Pits    Post holes    Ditches    Gullies/Beam-slots    Walls

FIGURE 1.20 The forum basilica and the sequence of Iron Age occupation and Roman timber buildings beneath it (adapted from Creighton with Fry 2016, fig. 5.31)

of, respectively, mid- and late 1st century date, predecessors of the eventual monumental masonry forum basilica which had been first discovered by Joyce (Fig. 1.20).

None of this sequence of buildings and occupation had been seriously damaged by the antiquarian excavations despite the building having been investigated for a second time by the Society of Antiquaries in 1892, as well as by earlier antiquarians before Joyce. What was very surprising was that, despite all previous interventions, late Roman occupation, shedding valuable light on how the building was used in the later 3rd and 4th centuries, survived intact at the northern end of the basilica. Surprising, too, was the resolution of a claim made by the Antiquaries' that, contrary to Joyce, and on the assumption of a particular symmetry along the long, north–south axis of the building, it contained two aisles, when it was abundantly clear (as it had been to Joyce) that there were only foundations for a single aisle. This was because the main focus of interest of the building was not north–south, but symmetrical about an east–west line between the monumental entrance to the forum on the eastern side and an apsidal chamber directly opposite in the west range of the complex. This room represented the shrine, the aedes, or sacred heart of the town.

## And then…

The hunch about the good survival of the early history of the town preserved beneath the masonry forum basilica had been proved correct, but did similar preservation exist elsewhere within the town where there was no monumental building to protect underlying deposits? Would it be possible to recover a complete history of the town from its Iron Age origins through to its demise after the end of Roman control of Britain at the beginning of the 5th century? What would be required to accomplish this? The state of knowledge about what to expect of excavating a Roman town in 1890 was such that it was considered practical to accomplish a 'total' excavation of the 100 or so acres within the town walls and within a reasonable timescale – 19 years as it turned out. By the end of the 20th century the amount of information that could be recovered from any excavation, but especially from an excavation within a Roman town, with its complex stratigraphy and abundance of finds, was of such a scale that an investigation of only a limited area of the town could be contemplated. But how large an area might be practicable? The 1980s excavation of the basilica, an area of only some 1200 m², gave a glimpse of the underlying late Iron Age occupation, and only part plans of the two periods of timber buildings sandwiched between the Iron Age and the construction of the overlying masonry forum basilica. Only total excavation beneath the masonry building would have given a reasonable prospect of recovering complete ground plans of those two timber buildings. However, with a depth of stratigraphy within the basilica of about a metre, it had taken some 28 weeks over seven summers with a team of

30–40 students and volunteers to complete that excavation as part of their training. Given that the basilica represented a little less than a sixth of the total area of the forum basilica, excavation of the entire building, including the forum piazza, at the same rate each year could have taken a further 35 years to complete!

Knowing this, we might wonder how long it might take to excavate totally – ie to the gravel subsoil – one complete insula of the town without public buildings, as a representative sample of the story of the town from beginning to end? Two sizes of block occupy the central area of the town, the larger of some 14,280 m², the smaller, of 9524 m², the one almost 12 times, the other almost eight times the area of the basilica excavation. To contemplate excavating either the larger or the smaller blocks, assuming the same depth of stratigraphy and employing the same number of volunteers, might require either about 84 or 56 seasons of excavation. Spread over a six- rather than a four-week summer season, a task of this magnitude would reduce the total number of seasons by a third, but the excavation would still take far too long. Alternatively, a programme of continuous excavation could reduce the task to between about seven and ten years, but at what cost? Whereas a training excavation with a force of students and volunteers carries a certain level of costs to sustain it, a full-time, continuous project would involve fulltime employment of a professional team and would cost many millions of pounds. It would then be followed by a post-excavation research and publication programme of corresponding scale and cost!

With such projections, the total excavation of a single insula would appear to be unattainable in a reasonable timescale without vast resources. This left the sampling of a block as the only realistic option. But how to choose one out of 37 blocks and then, within one, the particular area to excavate? In the event a project began in 1997 on part of Insula IX in the north-west quarter of the town (Fig. 1.21). This is one of the larger blocks, first investigated in 1893–4, and our excavation was to last 18 six-week long seasons, finishing in 2014. For about ten of those seasons it engaged as many as 150 students or volunteers on site at any one time and the annual cost was approximately £250,000. The area finally chosen was located in the northern half of the block and extended over 3025 m², about a quarter of the whole. It offered the potential of addressing a number of important questions about the development of the town.

An intriguing and long recognised aspect of the town plan is the number of buildings not aligned on the Roman street grid. These have been thought to relate to an early period in the town's history and further excavation in

FIGURE I.21 Insula
IX: aerial view of the
excavation in progress
in 2013

Insula IX would provide an opportunity to verify this. From the report published in 1895 it could be seen to include the footprint of one large, but poorly preserved town house, House I, aligned at 45° to the street grid, and one small building at right-angles to the main north–south street (Fig. 1.22). Research of the aerial photography in the early 1990s revealed the outline of another small building fronting onto the north–south street and a larger ground plan to the building previously discovered next to it compared with

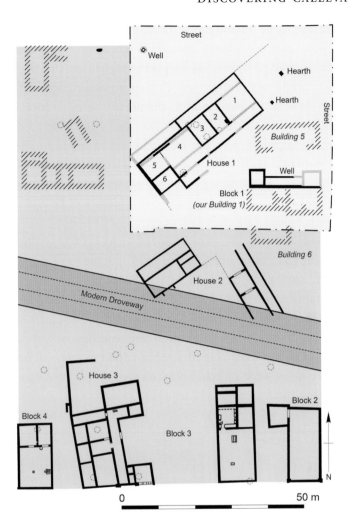

FIGURE 1.22 Insula IX: plan of the buildings discovered in 1893–4 and those (shaded) subsequently identified from aerial photography

what was originally reported. Finally, the area chosen was the findspot of one of the latest and most intriguing objects from the town, the celebrated Ogham stone (Chapter 9). Ogham is a form of written Celtic developed in southern Ireland around the turn of the 4th and 5th centuries AD. It uses letters of the Latin alphabet which have been converted into a system of markings which could be inscribed on stone or wood. The stone had been discovered in 1893 at the base of a pit or well dug through the foundations of House 1. Re-excavation might provide a better understanding of the context of this important find, deposited right at the end of the life of the Roman town.

Altogether the chosen area of Insula IX offered a mix of potential: the excavation of one previously unexplored building and part of a second, alongside the re-investigation of discoveries made in 1893–4. Apparently open spaces could be investigated for the remains of possible timber buildings. What was completely unknown was how well the underlying deposits were preserved and what they might yield of the late Iron Age and early Roman history of the town. Perhaps more important than all the above questions was the over-arching theme of the excavation. This was to trace how daily life changed over the 500 or so years of the occupation of the town. What might we learn of the changing accommodation, diet, dress, environment, identity, occupations, past times and ritual behaviour of the inhabitants? The discoveries which were eventually made and which have revolutionised our understanding of the town will be revealed in the chapters which follow.

At the same time as the excavation of Insula IX was ongoing, my colleagues John Creighton and Rob Fry used magnetometry to undertake a geophysical survey of the interior of the town and the immediate extramural landscape (Fig. 1.23). This method of prospection had taken off in the 1990s with a rapid development of equipment to meet the challenges of identifying potential archaeology across landscapes threatened by development. This survey has added much new information to our existing knowledge of extramural settlement and cemeteries as well

FIGURE 1.23 Comparative techniques: the forum area. Left: the Antiquaries' plan; centre: ground penetrating radar; right: magnetometry (fluxgate gradiometry) (Creighton with Fry 2016, fig. 4.3)

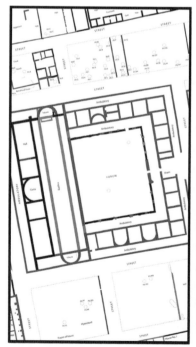

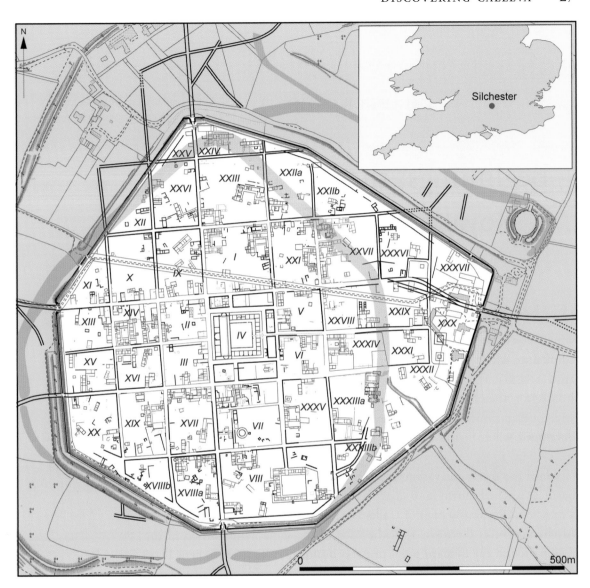

FIGURE 1.24 Plan of Iron Age and Roman Silchester consolidating the results from excavation, aerial photography and geophysical survey. The late Iron Age Inner Earthwork, which runs beneath the Roman town, is shown (adapted from Creighton with Fry 2016, folding plan)

as adding refinement to the plan of masonry-founded buildings within the town (Fig. 1.24).

Between the end of the Insula IX excavation in 2014 there has been further excavation, but of a much more targeted nature, which aims to reveal more of the early history of the town. Included in this work have been excavations on a possible early Roman bath complex in Insula III to the west of the forum, a temple in Insula XXX at the eastern end of the town and on the public baths in Insula XXXIII. The preliminary results of these projects will also be described in the following chapters.

# CHAPTER TWO

# Beginnings: the late Iron Age Royal Centre of Calleva

One of the most commonly asked questions about the Roman town is why it was located at Silchester and not on the Thames, for example at its confluence with the Kennet, where Reading is today (Fig. 2.1). The simple answer is that the Roman town was the successor to the preceding, late Iron Age, settlement but this merely invites the question as to why Calleva, which became one of the largest settlements of its time in southern Britain, developed where it did. We will return to this important question later (p. 47, Fig. 2.22).

Until the 1980s excavation beneath the great hall of the Roman forum basilica reached down and discovered the late Iron Age occupation, almost nothing was known of Calleva's origins. The Roman name, Calleva Atrebatum, links the town with the tribe of the same name settled in the region around the modern town of Arras in northern France, ancient Gaul (Fig. 2.2). The Atrebates enter the historical record during Julius Caesar's wars against the Gauls between 59 and 52 BC, when their leader, Commios, was, initially at least, a Roman ally. However, a later source, the Roman strategist Frontinus, describes how Commios escaped a pursuing Roman force and fled from Gaul to Britain, probably in about 50 BC, having fallen out with Caesar.

Coins were first introduced into Britain from Gaul before being produced locally. Examples which carry the legend Commios have been found in small numbers in central southern England and have been linked with the leader of the Atrebates (Fig. 2.3). Later, coins struck in gold and silver are known naming three individuals who claimed to be sons of Commios: Tincomarus,

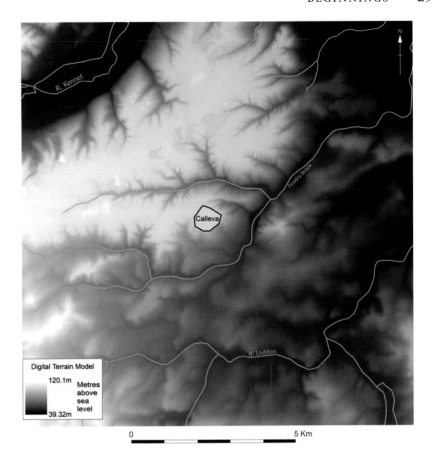

FIGURE 2.1 Between
Kennet and Loddon: a
Digital Terrain Model
locates Calleva on a
promontory on the
southern edge of the
higher (light shading)
ground of the Plateau
Gravels overlooking the
lower ground of the
Loddon valley (darker
shading)

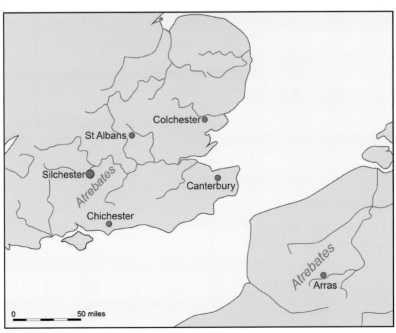

FIGURE 2.2 Map
showing the location
of major late Iron
Age towns (oppida)
in south-east England
and the homeland of
the Atrebates centred
on Arras in north-west
France

FIGURE 2.3
The distribution of
coins of Commios.
Top: a gold stater of
Commios
(© CHRIS RUDD LTD.
WWW.CELTICCOINS.COM)

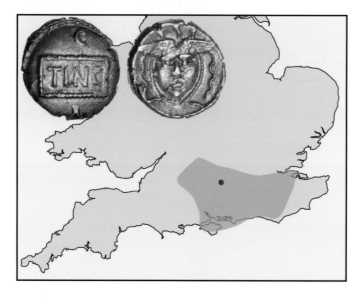

FIGURE 2.4
The distribution of
coins of Tincomarus.
Top: a gold quarter
stater of Tincomarus
(© CHRIS RUDD LTD.
WWW.CELTICCOINS.COM)

Eppillus and Verica (Figs 1.14, 2.4–2.5). Judging from the designs on his coins
Tincomarus seems to have been active from about 20 BC until displaced by
Eppillus in the first decade of the 1st century AD, with Verica succeeding
him by about AD 10. As well as Eppillus's coins carrying the title REX,
the Latin word for 'king', some also carry the legend CALLEV or CALLE,
the earliest (abbreviated) record of the place name Calleva, a Celtic word
meaning 'woodland place'. The identification of Calleva with Silchester
was finally confirmed beyond doubt by the discovery of an inscription

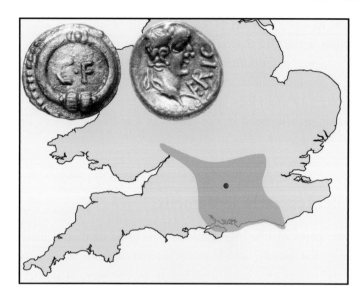

FIGURE 2.5
The distribution of
coins of Verica. Top: a
silver minim of Verica
from Insula IX

FIGURE 2.6
The distribution of
coins of Epatticus.
Top: a silver unit of
Epatticus
(© CHRIS RUDD LTD.
WWW.CELTICCOINS.COM)

containing the word CALLEVA, found within the Roman town in 1907 (Fig. 1.12). The distributions of the coins of the three Iron Age leaders have been equated with the territory of the kingdom of the Atrebates in Britain, though the later issues of Verica, after about AD 25, show a reduction in area to a territory centred on Chichester in West Sussex. Verica is linked with the 'Berikos' who appealed to the Emperor Claudius to restore his kingdom to him, having been driven out, it is thought, by the expansion of the Catuvellauni, a major tribal confederacy, centred on Camulodunum

(Colchester) in Essex and led by Cunobelin until his death about AD 40. The reduction in the area covered by the later issues of Verica coincided with the spread of coins of Cunobelin's brother, Epatticus, over the northern half of what had previously been seen to be part of the Atrebatic kingdom (Fig. 2.6). This territory included Calleva. At the time of the Roman Conquest Calleva seems to have been in the hands of Caratacus, one of the sons of Cunobelin (Chapter 3).

## Early defences, early settlement

What do we know of Iron Age Calleva? The great bank and ditch, George Boon's Inner Earthwork, which encircles the settlement, is now scarcely visible to the naked eye, but immediately to the west of it there are two stretches of surviving rampart and ditch. One is to the north-west, next to Rye House, where the bank still survives to a height of about 2 m above the present ground surface, the other is in Rampier's Copse to the south-west, where the rampart is much more massive, rising to a height of 3.5–5 m, where it incorporates part of the bank of a small, earlier Iron Age enclosure (Fig. 2.7). Calleva was particularly vulnerable to attack from the level ground to the west and both these surviving earthworks were perhaps intended to provide defence from attack from that direction. But there are puzzling features about both: not only do the two ramparts not join up, but the Rampier Copse bank tails off to the north-west, on a different alignment

FIGURE 2.7 The Iron Age ditch and rampart in Rampiers Copse

(DP218210 © HISTORIC ENGLAND ARCHIVE, PHOTOGRAPH STEVE BAKER)

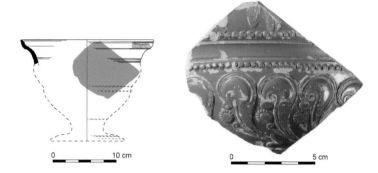

FIGURE 2.8 A fragment of a relief-decorated Arretine crater from Insula IX made by the potter Cn Ateius Xanthus at a workshop at Pisa, north Italy, *c.* 5 BC–*c.* AD 20

to that of its counterpart to the north-east. Likewise, the latter tails away before it reaches the edge of the promontory where the ground drops away to the north and east. Other than offering a degree of cover to approaches from the west these earthworks otherwise appear unconnected and perhaps unfinished. There is no reliable evidence with which to date them, but they are likely to be Iron Age, though probably not as late as the Inner Earthwork.

The Antiquaries admitted defeat as far as gaining any insight into Iron Age Calleva. Within the Roman walls they had found mixed with Roman material some Iron Age coins and artefacts pre-dating the Roman conquest of Britain of AD 43, including sherds of a distinctive imported pottery from the Roman world, a fine red gloss tableware made at Arezzo in northern Italy and known as Arretine (Fig. 2.8). This type of pottery reached British shores in small quantities between about 10 BC and AD 20, but none of these antiquarian finds from Calleva was excavated from a late Iron Age context. More helpfully, George Boon's discovery and investigation in the 1950s of the great defensive enclosure, which he called the 'Inner Earthwork,' had showed that it enclosed a huge area, about 38 hectares (83 acres) and almost exactly coincident with the area of the later Roman town (Fig. 2.9). From its size alone it might reasonably be inferred that Calleva was a major settlement of the late Iron Age of southern Britain. Boon dated the enclosure to around AD 25–50, in other words shortly before the Roman invasion, though subsequent work has suggested it could date from as early as 20–10 BC and the start of the late Iron Age settlement.

Of the nature of the settlement inside the enclosure nothing was known before the 1980s when the excavation beneath the Roman forum basilica revealed the remains of two metalled lanes or streets aligned north-west to south-east and north-east to south-west, flanked by stout fences inside each of which was a neat row of rubbish pits. Within the limited area contained

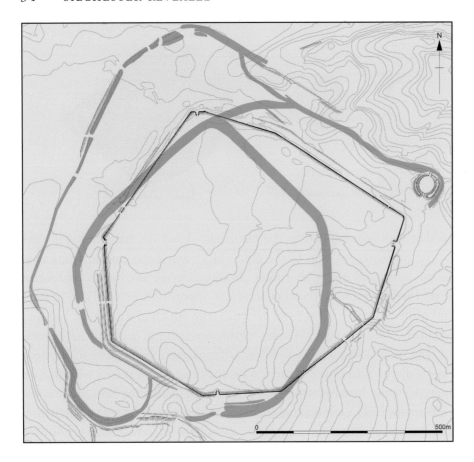

FIGURE 2.9 Plan of the Iron Age defences of Calleva (after Creighton with Fry 2016, fig. 9.3)

by the foundations of the Roman basilica there was little space in which to find evidence of the character of contemporary buildings but traces of both round and rectangular structures were found. Water was supplied from wells. On the basis of both imported wine-carrying amphoras and Iron Age coins, occupation appeared to be no earlier than about 20 BC, though excavation of the larger area in what became Insula IX of the Roman town suggested a slightly later start date, from about 10 BC. These dates are therefore somewhat distant from the time of Commios's flight from Gaul and, at present, there is nothing that has been found within the Inner Earthwork of Calleva with which to fill an interval of about 40 years. Yet the distribution of Commios's coins and an earlier, uninscribed series centres more or less on Calleva. Given how little has so far been explored of Iron Age Calleva, evidence of Commios's stronghold may yet emerge. Nevertheless, we may wonder whether Tincomarus, Eppillus and Verica really were sons of Commios.

Our sense that the start of Calleva had little to do with the immediate history of settlement in the surrounding area is in keeping with what is currently known within a 1–2 mile (1.6–3.2 km) radius of the promontory defended by the Inner Earthwork. Recent excavations in 2015–2017 show occupation of middle Iron Age date (4th–2nd century BC), of enclosed settlements to the north near Simm's Copse and at Pond Farm, Mortimer West End, the latter site with its defensive bank and ditch still well preserved on the north and west sides, as well as south-west of Calleva in Pamber Forest, but no evidence of continuation to the late Iron Age and the time of Calleva. Only the settlement at Windabout Copse, Mortimer shows evidence of occupation contemporary with that within the Inner Earthwork (Fig. 2.10). Against this background it is hard to see Calleva emerging as a nucleation deriving from either an initiative by Commios or an increase in the density of surrounding settlements. On the contrary, as we shall see, the character of the occupation suggests a new foundation, one primarily of colonists from northern France.

FIGURE 2.10 Plan of the cropmarks of the Iron Age farmstead and burial enclosure at Windabout, south of Mortimer

## The earliest inhabitants

The larger area afforded by the excavation at Insula IX has confirmed the preliminary conclusion of the earlier excavation beneath the forum basilica that the area within the Inner Earthwork was divided up into compounds separated from each other by lanes on a grid roughly aligned north-east to south-west and north-west to south-east. The greatest area of compound exposed (the Central Compound in Insula IX), contained a large timber hall, 47.5 m in length and 7.5 m in width, with smaller rectangular buildings, also of timber, around it to the north (Figs 2.11–2.13). It was built at right-angles to the adjacent trackway on a north-east to south-west orientation. The significance of this alignment is explored further in Chapter 5. Given its size the hall is interpreted as the residence of one of the leading men of the Atrebates and, just as was the case with the excavation beneath the forum basilica, the finds from the associated rubbish pits and abandoned wells hint at the high status and relative wealth of the occupants. Buried in the foundation trench were the remains of a miniature dog, one of the earliest examples of such a breed found in Britain (see Fig. 1.19). As we saw in Chapter 1, analysis of the isotopes of oxygen and strontium suggests that the dog was imported from the continent. Prominent among the other finds is the imported pottery, including fragments of the large transport vessels (amphorae) carrying wine, olive oil and other foodstuffs from the west Mediterranean world, especially from Italy, southern France and southern Spain (Fig. 2.14). There was complementary table ware, mostly the fine, red-slipped cups and platters, but also fragments of large relief-decorated bowls, from the arretine factories of Italy and Lyon in France (Fig. 2.8). Even greater quantities of drinking vessels and tableware, the latter imitating the Mediterranean styles, but with black as well as red-slipped surfaces, were imported from northern France, much of it from potteries in the region around Reims (see Fig. 2.20). Remarkably, some cooking ware was also imported, in this case from the Auvergne region of central France. Eating off platters, rather than from bowls, and drinking from cups or larger beakers points to very different social practice to that found on Iron Age settlements elsewhere across the countryside of southern Britain. Rare finds also include imported glass of which the bowls cast from polychrome canes fused together are particularly fine. They were probably made in Italy.

Like the pottery, the remains of the actual foodstuffs which were found are distinctively different in character to those found in Iron Age settlements elsewhere in southern Britain. While the charred remains of the staples of

FIGURE 2.11 Aerial view of Insula IX in 2013–14 showing the character of the late Iron Age and earliest Roman occupation; the construction trenches of the Iron Age hall are clearly visible running diagonally across the image. Compere this with Figs 2.12 and 2.13

FIGURE 2.12 Aerial view of Insula IX looking north-east and showing the outline of the late Iron Age hall. Compare with Figs 2.11 and 2.13

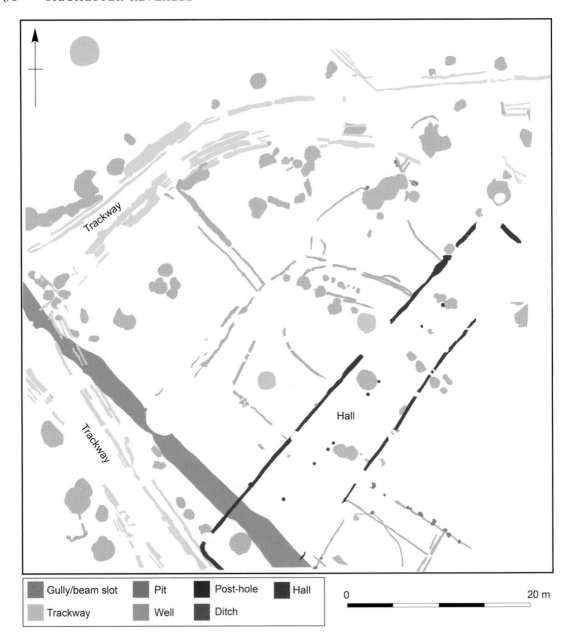

Trackway

Trackway

Hall

| | Gully/beam slot | | Pit | | Post-hole | | Hall |
| | Trackway | | Well | | Ditch | | |

0                                                                    20 m

wheat and barley are common across the excavated area, waterlogged deposits from Calleva contained flavourings of celery, coriander and dill which are typical of Mediterranean cuisine. The earliest olives, an important aspect of diet in the Classical world, so far found in Britain were also preserved in these deposits. There is also evidence for the consumption of pulses such as the garden pea and seeds of the oil crop, flax. The inhabitants also

FIGURE 2.13 Plan of the excavated area of Insula IX showing the character of the late Iron Age occupation. Compare with Figs 2.11 and 2.12

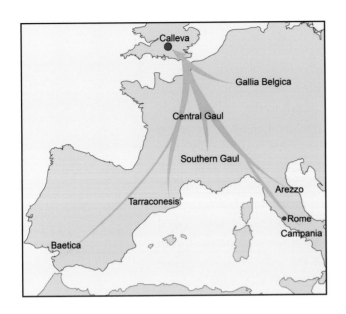

FIGURE 2.14 Map showing sources of the continental and Mediterranean imports found in late Iron Age Calleva

had a meat-rich diet with beef the most popular followed by lamb or mutton and then pork. Chicken was also eaten and both horse and dog were occasionally consumed. This also appears to be the case with wild animals, such as deer, birds and fish. The importance of meat in the diet is re-inforced by the analysis of the residues from cooking preserved on the internal surfaces of pottery vessels. This has shown that beef or mutton were most commonly consumed but there were also indications of other types of meat including, possibly, pork. Once again, the preference for beef and the evidence from the residues in the cooking pots for the processing of meat rather than of milk and dairy products distinguishes Calleva from other contemporary settlements in southern Britain. Finally, and particularly from the forum basilica site rather than from Insula IX, there are the remains of shellfish, mostly oysters, but some mussels too, presumably imported from the Solent or the Thames Estuary.

Getting closer to the inhabitants of Calleva, other than through their food and the manner in which they ate and drank, is hard because of what little survives, particularly of organic materials, in the archaeological record. We have no clear idea of what people wore other than that garments like tunics and cloaks would have been of wool. Brooches were numerous and valued as important for fastening and decorating clothing. Surprisingly, those forged out of iron are relatively common and quite likely manufactured in Calleva but there is a greater number made of copper alloy and, while some are clearly imports either from the continent or from elsewhere in southern Britain, others were also probably made and sold in the settlement. They are quite slight items, typically no more than 7 cm in length, suitable perhaps for fastening only light items of clothing. More surprising is the presence of quantities of iron hobnails from leather footwear, the leather long since decayed. Since we do not yet have evidence for tanning technology in Iron Age Britain, the footwear must have been imported. Was this just another traded item, or is it further evidence of incomers, such as traders, or, as nailed footwear was closely associated with the Roman military, of soldiers in the settlement?

# Crafts and agriculture

If the detritus of high living dominates the archaeological record, there is also evidence of other activities taking place within Calleva. Most significant of these and consistent with the high status we attach to the settlement was the production of precious metal coinage of gold and silver. The casting of plain discs of the metals in fired clay 'pellet moulds' was an early stage of the process before they were struck to make the actual coins (Fig. 2.15). Fragments of these moulds have been found in both the forum basilica and, widely and thinly distributed, the Insula IX excavation, but fragments of crucibles for the initial melting of the metals have only been found concentrated in the centre, from the Iron Age occupation beneath the forum basilica. This might suggest that the minting of the coins took place close by. Only Eppillus struck coins with the legend CALLE, CALLEV, but it is highly likely that Tincomarus and Verica also struck some of their coinage at Calleva.

Copper alloy was also cast in pre-fabricated fired clay moulds to make decorative items of horse harness and chariot fittings. This activity was revealed by the find of a large deposit of broken moulds and crucibles in a rubbish pit beneath the forum basilica along with the complete skeleton of an adult man, perhaps the bronze smith himself. The singularity of this find suggests that is likely to have been the waste of an itinerant smith, though the incidence of copper alloy brooches, as mentioned above, suggests that there were probably resident metalworkers making some of these as well, but working from pre-prepared metal sheet and wire. Iron, too, was both smelted in small quantities in shallow, bowl-shaped hearths and forged into artefacts at Calleva. These would have included the brooches mentioned above and also a range of tools for activities like carpentry and textile-working as well as a variety of miscellaneous fittings. Iron artefacts of this date are not common but they include finds like styli for writing on wooden tablets, occasional agricultural tools, and items associated with transport and weapons. Neither of the two excavations which have so

FIGURE 2.15 Piece of a late Iron Age fired clay pellet-mould from Insula IX

0            50 mm

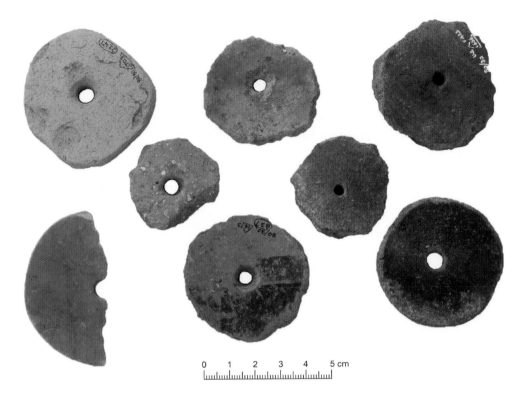

FIGURE 2.16 A group of late Iron Age and early Roman spindle whorls fashioned out of sherds of pottery

far revealed the late Iron Age settlement produced such quantities of the waste from iron smelting or smithing as to indicate a particular focus for these activities.

Among other occupations, the finds of textile equipment, particularly spindle whorls, attest the spinning and then, no doubt, the weaving of wool, while needles point to the sewing of garments (Fig. 2.16).

Farming was almost certainly a major activity. The weed seeds associated with deposits of charred barley and wheat found in the rubbish pits and abandoned wells suggest that the cereals were grown on local soils within easy reach of the settlement, for example from farms like that at Windabout, and not from as far as the not-so-distant chalkland soils of the Berkshire Downs to the north or the Hampshire Downs south. The evidence of insects which thrive on animal dung indicates that animals were grazed within or close to the Central Compound and deposits of stable-flooring material suggest that some, probably horses, were kept within the settlement, while the identification of hay indicates a source of food for them. This find is a rare and early indicator of hay meadow management in Britain.

# Trade networks

What can we conclude about late Iron Age Calleva? It was the centre from which the likes of Tincomarus, Eppillus and Verica controlled the larger territory of the Atrebates, which their coins suggest extended over much of central southern England south of the Thames, at least until the reign of Verica, when Calleva and the northern part of the kingdom appear to have been taken over by the Catuvellaunian Epatticus. The settlement was the focal point of extensive trade networks both within southern Britain and across the Channel to northern France and southwards to the Mediterranean. The importation of wine, olives, olive oil and other foodstuffs, in a variety of containers including transport amphorae, as well as tableware pottery, has already been mentioned, but other finds help illustrate the widespread nature of the contacts. First, Iron Age coins, where a considerable number of those found at Calleva were struck by tribes in northern, or Belgic Gaul (France), from the areas around Amiens, Cambrai, Reims and Soissons, and which further illustrate the strength of contacts with that region. There are also finds from Armorica (Brittany), from the region around Besançon in the centre, and one from the distant tribe of the Volcae Arecomici located in the south of France. Within Britain, not surprisingly, we have representation of the silver issues of Tincomarus, Eppillus and Verica, but there are greater numbers of coins from the Eastern Region. These are represented by the less

FIGURE 2.17 Map showing Calleva's principal links across southern Britain

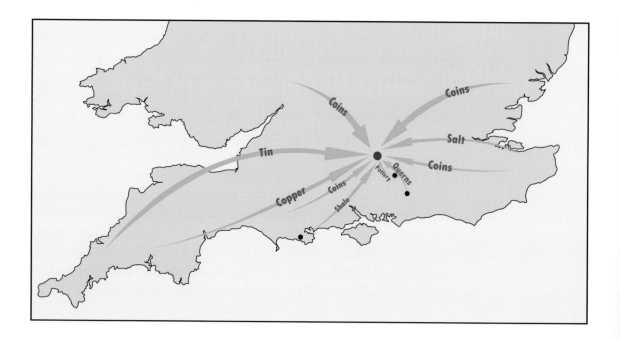

valuable, bronze coins of Tasciovanus and Cunobelin. Together, they imply strong connections across the Thames and to the heart of the Catuvellaunian kingdom centred on Camulodunum (Colchester), but there are also links with Kent to the east as well as to the west, the Severn-Cotswold region, the territory of the Dobunni, and south-west to Dorset, the land of the Durotriges.

Other categories of artefact also show a diversity of connections (Fig. 2.17). Eastward to the Thames Estuary and the north Kent coast we have the source of salt which was brought to Calleva in containers made in a distinctive type of pottery called briquetage. To the south, to West Sussex, we find the stone quarries at Lodsworth which were the source of the great majority of the querns (handmills) used to grind Calleva's corn into flour (Fig. 2.18). To the south-west of Calleva we have the source of the shale used for personal adornment (armlets, bracelets) and tableware (platters) at Kimmeridge, on the Isle of Purbeck in south-east Dorset. Further to the south-west likely sources for the tin and part-smelted copper found at the forum basilica site are Cornwall and Devon. Apart from some pottery drinking vessels which may have been made near Abingdon about 25 miles north of Calleva, where many examples have been found, there is little evidence of any links, other than through the coins already mentioned, to the north of the River Thames. There is a single example of a handmade pottery cauldron which is only paralleled by finds from the South Midlands (Fig. 2.19).

It is unlikely that, other than the continental and Mediterranean imports, what survives archaeologically is truly representative not only of the goods which were traded into the settlement, but, above all, of what was traded in exchange. What did Calleva give in return for the imported goods we find there? One ancient source, the geographer Strabo writing about

0    1    2 cm

FIGURE 2.19
A unique find:
a late Iron Age
shell-tempered
pottery vessel
imported to
Calleva from the
south Midlands
region, shaped
in the form of a
bronze cauldron

20 BC, offers a clue. Britain, he says, produces grain and cattle, gold, silver and iron. These were exported along with hides and slaves and dogs bred specifically for hunting. Such things, and such people, are very hard to trace in the archaeological record, most being organic perishables and raw materials, but it seems that they were exchanged for luxury manufactured goods and foodstuffs from the continent and the Mediterranean world. We can imagine that Calleva was the hub to which those kinds of goods which Strabo lists were brought and then re-exported either via the Thames or the south coast across the Channel to Gaul. If we are correct that Calleva was taken over by the Catuvellaunian kingdom after c. AD 25, it is possible that some of this trade passed through, or was even consumed at, Camulodunum (Colchester, Essex).

The regions in Britain where we can identify links with Calleva by virtue of the survival of certain artefacts can also be seen as the likely source of some those raw materials and commodities which the Roman world was keen to acquire. In this context we may interpret the distribution of Atrebatic gold and silver coins, the latter certainly, the gold probably, made from recycled

FIGURE 2.20 Pottery vessels deposited as grave goods with a cremation burial dated to around the time of the Roman conquest of AD 43 found at Windabout, Mortimer, on the Hampshire–Berkshire border. The pair of cups and the pair of platters in the upper half of the picture were made near Reims in northern France; the four platters below are copies of the imported vessels and made locally near Calleva

metal from the Roman world, across central southern Britain as payments to those who furnished the required goods, thus securing their loyalty to the king. In addition, small quantities of the imported luxury goods also found their way into the countryside, but the great majority were consumed at Calleva. A rich grave associated with the farmstead at Windabout, only about 1 km east of Calleva, contained an assemblage of eight pottery vessels of which half, two platters and two cups, were examples of the imports from northern Gaul so well represented at Calleva itself (Fig. 2.20). At Latchmere Green another rich late Iron Age cremation burial of an adult and a young child was found in 1994. It was furnished with a finely engraved bronze mirror of British manufacture, described at the time of its discovery as 'perhaps the subtlest of all known British mirrors' (Fig. 2.21).

At first sight Calleva does not seem well placed to articulate this trade with the Roman world, but its location is within 10 miles (c. 16 km) of the confluence of the rivers Thames and Kennet, their valleys and waterways offering the possibilities of moving further into the interior of southern Britain: on the one hand, north into Oxfordshire and Gloucestershire and, on the other, westwards into Wiltshire and the regions further west and

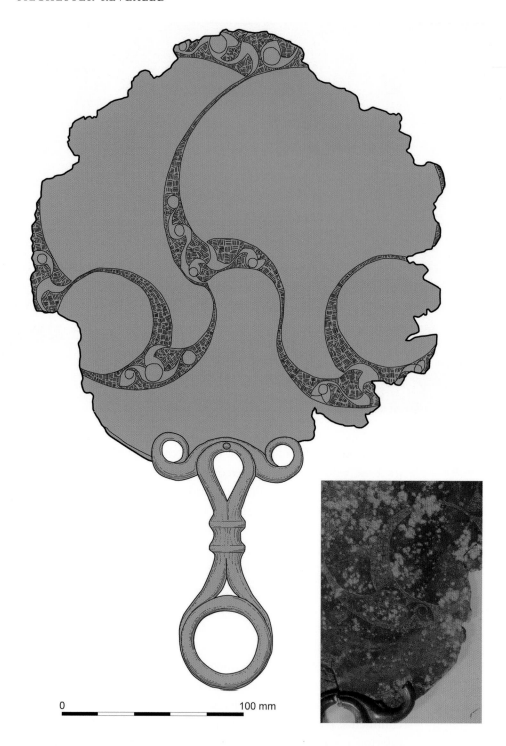

FIGURE 2.21 Latchmere Green, Hampshire: drawing of the late Iron Age mirror associated with a cremation burial of an adult and child. Note the detail of its intricate, engraved design

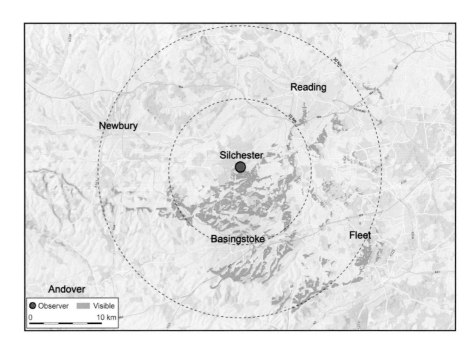

FIGURE 2.22
The highlighted areas show an observer could see landscape features more than 12.5 miles (20 km) distant to the south on a clear day when standing on the late Iron Age rampart by the South Gate

south-west. Looking the other way, the Thames offered a key conduit for carrying trade to and from the estuary and across the North Sea and Channel to northern Gaul. While logic might have suggested the actual confluence of Thames and Kennet at Reading as the best location for a trading settlement, the promontory on which Calleva was established was eminently defensible on all sides except the west and its relative height gave it a clear view to the south for a dozen miles or so across the landscape to the Hampshire Downs (Fig. 2.22). It was also located in a landscape which, though occupied earlier in the Iron Age, appears to have been relatively empty and, as its name suggests, relatively wooded in the late 1st century BC.

## Calleva in context

How might we imagine Calleva appeared on the eve of the Roman Conquest in AD 43? Within the massive defences of the Inner Earthwork we may reconstruct a settlement divided into compounds separated from one another by a network of lanes broadly oriented north-east to south-west and north-west to south-east. If the Central Compound discovered in Insula IX is representative, then the other compounds were also each occupied by a great timber hall to accommodate a leading member of the tribe, with

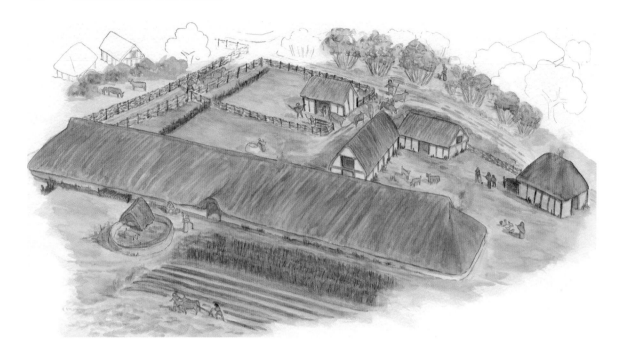

FIGURE 2.23
Reconstruction of the
excavated area of Insula
IX in the late Iron Age
(by Margaret Mathews).
View to the north with
the great hall in the
foreground and the two
trackways bounding the
compound

smaller timber buildings housing their dependants and slaves clustered around (Figs 2.23–2.24). Judging by differences in the range and quantity of luxury goods and the higher status occupations evidenced in the centre of the settlement, we might propose that there were different arrangements of buildings there to accommodate the king and his retinue of supporters.

Calleva was one of a handful of settlements in south-east Britain which shared similar characteristics in terms of their finds, most recognisably in a significant representation of imported ceramic tableware and amphorae from exactly the same sources: pre-eminently from northern Gaul but also, more distantly, from the Mediterranean world of the south of France, Italy and southern Spain. These settlements include Canterbury, Chichester, Colchester and Verulamium, all of which, like Calleva, became major Roman towns. Of these, it is Colchester, the British Camulodunum, which we know most about from extensive excavations in the 1930s and it offers the closest parallel to Calleva.

As we have seen with the evidence from Calleva, these settlements are completely different in character from their contemporaries in the larger landscape of south-east England. They all emerge at the same time, with trade and exchange with the Roman world as their *raison d'être*. The very strong connections with the tribes of northern Gaul suggest that the initiative to establish these settlements in south-east England lay with them,

FIGURE 2.24
Reconstruction of late
Iron Age Calleva near
the South Gate. Note
the mix of round and
rectangular buildings
(© HISTORIC ENGLAND ARCHIVE)

their leaders and Roman merchants. The time when they were established at the end of the 1st century BC coincides with the intensive campaigning by the Roman army across the Rhine into Germania. Those campaigns would have required considerable supplies to support them and this may be why the opportunity was seized to gain control of the procurement of British foodstuffs and raw materials. Since Gaul was under Roman control it is unlikely that the initiative to plant settlements in south-east England was undertaken without the knowledge and, perhaps also, the support of the Roman authorities. Indeed, it is not unreasonable to suppose that the common find of iron hobnails from Iron Age Calleva may be equated with soldiers' boots. Although the historian Dio Cassius, writing in the later 2nd and early 3rd century AD, records that the Emperor Augustus made plans for the further conquest of Britain early on in his reign, in 34, 27 and 26 BC, these do not appear to have ever been implemented. Instead, what we find is that a series of entrepôts, of which Calleva was one, were set up, perhaps with the support of the Roman military, north and south of the middle and lower Thames in south-east England by about 10 BC. At the

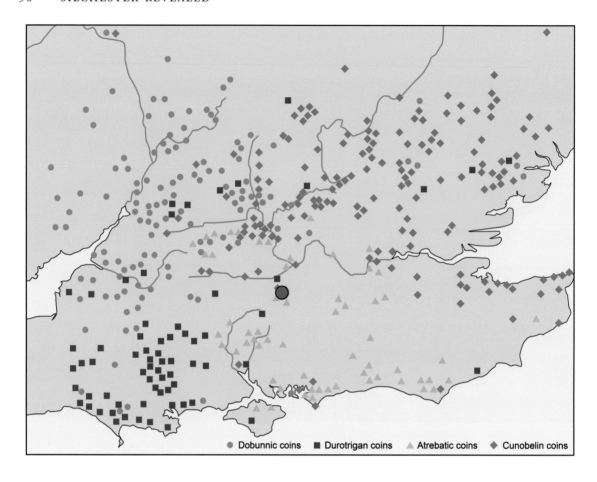

● Dobunnic coins   ■ Durotrigan coins   ▲ Atrebatic coins   ◆ Cunobelin coins

interface of the distributions of Catuvellaunian, Dobunnic and Atrebatic coins, Calleva's position can be seen as central to this exploitation of the resources of southern Britain (Fig. 2.25).

While Calleva is seen as the centre of a 'Southern Kingdom' of the Atrebates, that of Tincomarus and his successors, Camulodunum is regarded as at the heart of an 'Eastern Kingdom' of the Catuvellauni headed by Cunobelin. As we have seen, the coins of his brother Epatticus suggest the more powerful Eastern Kingdom annexed Calleva and its networks, so becoming the most powerful political entity in southern Britain. It is no surprise that it was to Camulodunum that the invasion forces of Claudius marched in AD 43, leaving the taking of Calleva to the following year.

FIGURE 2.25 Calleva at the hub of the coin distributions of the major political groupings in central southern Britain

# CHAPTER THREE

# Caratacus, the Roman conquest, Nero and Calleva

In this chapter we explore how Calleva changed in the decades immediately following the Roman invasion of AD 43 when the Emperor Claudius ordered his army to invade Britain. The immediate objective was Camulodunum (Colchester), the centre of the kingdom of Cunobelin and his heirs, Caratacus and Togodumnus. Although the invading army eventually consisted of four legions and an equivalent force of auxiliaries, we do not know how long it took to land them or whether there was capacity to do more than cross the Thames and take Camulodunum in what was left of the campaigning season of AD 43. Evidence from Alchester, Oxfordshire, about 85 miles (137 km) west of Camulodunum and about 35 miles (56 km) due north of Calleva, indicates fortress building there by the autumn of the following year and it is also likely that Calleva came under Roman control that summer of AD 44. The association was noted in the previous chapter with Caratacus, one of the sons of Cunobelin, who we know from the accounts of the Roman historian, Tacitus, continued to resist the Roman army until he was betrayed in AD 51 by Cartimandua of the Brigantes, a northern British tribe. This suggests the likelihood that the taking of Calleva was resisted.

The connection of Caratacus with Calleva is, as with previous rulers, through his coins whose distribution is centred on Calleva (Fig. 3.1). With its network of route ways leading into the western hinterland, Calleva was already an important communication hub by the time of the Roman invasion and an obvious point from which to resist the advancing Roman forces. It is quite possible that the massive defensive earthwork (the Inner Earthwork of Chapter 2) was constructed at this time to defend Calleva from Roman assault (Fig. 3.2). Although in one excavated section what remained of the rampart was found to overlie pottery that could date as early as 20–10 BC, pottery discarded into the bottom of the associated ditch dates much later, to the mid-1st century AD. This implies that, if not actually built from scratch around the time of the conquest, the ditch of the already existing defence was, at the very least, cleaned out then and the extracted material presumably used to heighten and refurbish the rampart.

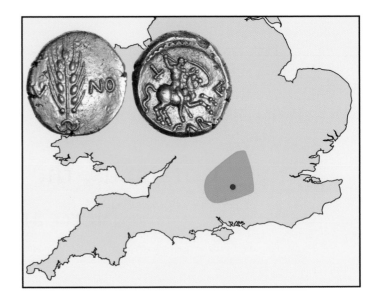

A notable feature of this earthwork was that, with its wide, flat-bottomed ditch, it was designed to trap Roman assault artillery at such a distance from the rampart that it could be attacked by the defenders on the rampart above. Only very slight traces now remain of that rampart, so we cannot know whether it was slighted by Roman invasion forces, but the lowest layers of the ditch in the very limited areas which have been excavated have produced fragments of human skulls (Fig. 3.3). Further human remains, including the complete skeleton of a young adult, as well as the remains of perhaps five others, have also been found in the pits and ditches flanking the late Iron Age trackways beneath the forum basilica that were filled around the time of

FIGURE 3.1 The distribution of coins of Caratacus. Top: unique gold stater of Caratacus
(© CHRIS RUDD LTD. WWW.CELTICCOINS.COM)

FIGURE 3.2 The late Iron Age Inner Earthwork: a section of the ditch, 4 m deep at this point, under excavation next to the later, Roman public baths in 2019; from above (right); in profile (left)

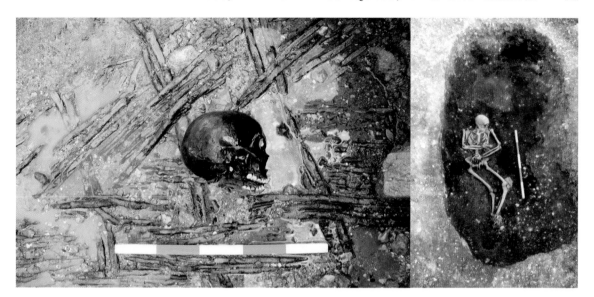

FIGURE 3.3 Burials from around the time of the Roman conquest, AD 43/44: left: the skull of a young adult male carefully laid to rest on a wattle stretcher towards the base of the Inner Earthwork ditch next to the Roman baths; right: the skeleton of a young adult male from a late Iron Age pit beneath the forum basilica

the conquest. Further human remains have also been found in Insula IX and in the 1991 excavations at the North Gate, including a femur with cut and chop marks, which is radiocarbon dated to the Iron Age (Fig. 3.4). Could all these be the remains of victims of the Roman assault on Caratacus's stronghold, or even of earlier struggles for control of Calleva?

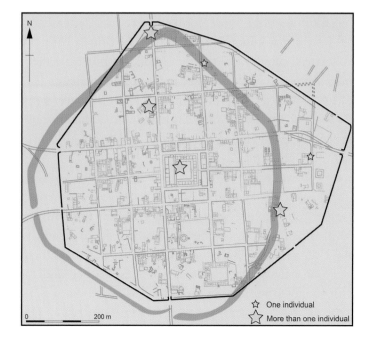

FIGURE 3.4 Distribution of late Iron Age human remains at Calleva, including those dating to around the time of the Roman conquest

What of a Roman assault? Do we have evidence of an early military presence in Calleva? While no trace has yet been found of a formally organised Roman fort or fortress, there are many finds of broken Roman armour and weaponry from both the modern excavations which have explored the entire occupational sequence down to the geological subsoil, that beneath the forum basilica and the large, area investigation at Insula IX. Although it is not possible to associate these pieces with a particular year, they are found in contexts which date to the time of the conquest and the years immediately following. The legion that is most likely to have been responsible for the taking of Calleva was the Second Augustan Legion commanded by its legate, Vespasian, who later became Emperor of Rome in AD 69. In the account of his life, the historian Suetonius records the legion's defeat of two powerful, but unnamed tribes, the taking of more than 20 towns (oppida) and the conquest of the Isle of Wight. Calleva could well have been one of those 20 towns. Strategically, it was probably the most important.

The Roman presence at Calleva developed quite differently from the occupation of Camulodunum. There a more permanent military occupation took shape with the construction of a fortress for the Twentieth Legion next to the late Iron Age settlement at Sheepen. In contrast, the military occupation of Calleva appears to have been short-lived, the soldiers making use of existing buildings in the settlement rather than constructing anything of a recognisably military character, such as barrack blocks or granaries. The lack of a need for anything more permanent chimes with what we know of the rapid pace of the conquest of the south of Britain with evidence of a legionary fortress, presumably for the Second Legion, at Lake, north of Poole, Dorset from the mid-/late 40s and a replacement for it at Exeter, built about 10 years later. The military presence was, however, long enough to have had an influence on diet as reflected by the dominance of cattle, as opposed to sheep or goat, among the remains of the animals consumed and deposited in the rubbish pits.

We can only presume that the population of Calleva fled or was enslaved when it was taken by Vespasian's forces and that people only returned when the army moved on. Around this time there is hint of disruption in the pollen record, which indicates some regeneration of shrub and woodland at the expense of cereals cultivated in the fields around the settlement, but such regeneration takes some years to become established and there is no evidence that the town was empty for as long as, say, 5 years.

# An unusual building

In disentangling the story of the earliest years of the Roman occupation of Calleva, there is a further strand to explore. Beneath the forum basilica and overlying the late Iron Age occupation, which contained the human remains described above, substantial timber buildings, quite unlike any so far associated with Calleva, were constructed in the mid-/late 40s (Fig. 3.5). They were oriented north–south/east–west and overlay the quite differently oriented trackways of the Iron Age settlement. The complex consisted of at least two buildings, with hints of a third, one of which was almost completely excavated. Anticipating the layout of future buildings on this site we have reconstructed them as part of a single entity composed of four ranges set around a central courtyard. Excavation revealed the care with which the buildings had been constructed with deep, vertical-sided, foundation trenches dug to carry the sleeper beams which supported the vertical components of the buildings. The latter survived as voids, rectangular in cross-section, where the timbers had decayed.

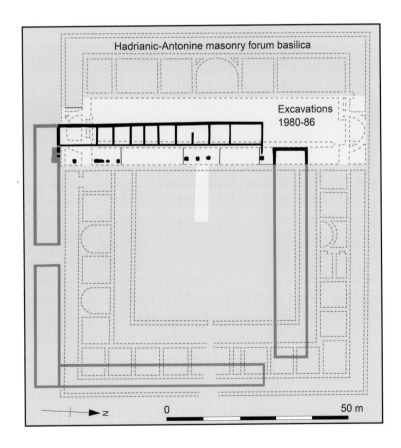

FIGURE 3.5 A conjectural plan of the Claudian 'courtyard building' found beneath the masonry forum basilica at the heart of Calleva

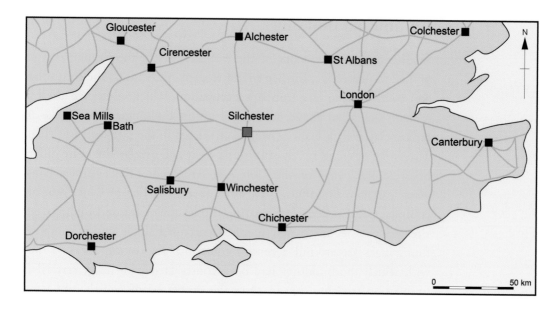

FIGURE 3.6 Calleva at the hub of a network of major Roman roads

With its very distinctive form of construction, it was initially interpreted as the headquarters building of a Roman fort or fortress, but with the absence of evidence of further military buildings from the extensive Insula IX excavation, other ideas, such as that it may have been designed as the first forum (market place) of the town, have been suggested. Even with further work to explore the other ranges of the building we may never be confident of an interpretation of this, so far, unique building complex. However, as the character of its build suggests, it was undoubtedly an officially inspired construction and this is underlined both by the way it completely ignores the topography of the existing settlement and by the finds of Roman military equipment associated with it. Its location next to what became the principal thoroughfares of the Roman town is also probably significant (Fig. 3.6). Immediately to the north was what became the east–west street which carried all the traffic from London to the west country and south Wales, the road dividing some miles west of the town near Newbury. From there one branch led due west towards Bath and the crossing of the Severn Estuary at Sea Mills and the other north-west to Cirencester and Gloucester. Just to the west of it was the street which led north to Dorchester-on-Thames and Alchester, and south to Chichester and Winchester, the road dividing just south of the town at Latchmere Green. Like Calleva, both these latter towns became tribal capitals under the Roman administration. With a further road leading south-west towards Salisbury, Dorchester and, ultimately, Exeter, Calleva was at the hub of a network of major Roman roads, some or all of which may have followed the course of late Iron Age routeways.

Assuming that the 'courtyard building' was not connected to the immediate conquest of Calleva and its adjacent territories, its relationship to these major roads may provide a further clue to a different role linked with the development of London and the latter's role as the logistical heart of the conquest of Britain. We know that Ostorius Scapula, the second governor of Britain (AD 47–52), was active with the Twentieth Legion against the Silures in south Wales while, as we have seen, the Second Legion, initially under the command of Vespasian, was occupied in the pacification of the Durotriges and the Dumnonii in the south-west. Calleva would have been busy with troops and supplies passing through it, and a major building in a central location within the town, acting as an early form of mansio (inn) to support those movements of men and materials, makes very good sense (Fig. 3.7) Tantalising foundations of an early brick-built structure have recently been found on the site of the later, public baths. These may be the remains of an early bath house, an essential comfort to support the Roman officials occupying the central 'courtyard building'.

With an official Roman building next to two arterial roads crossing at right-angles and overlying the lanes and trackways of Iron Age Calleva, is it reasonable to suppose that the town remained under Roman military control, even if it was not occupied by a large garrison? It had been at the heart of the kingdom of Verica and his predecessors, but then there is the evidence of a Catuvellaunian takeover, first by Epatticus and then by Caratacus, who we know opposed the Roman invasion, including at Calleva itself, as we have

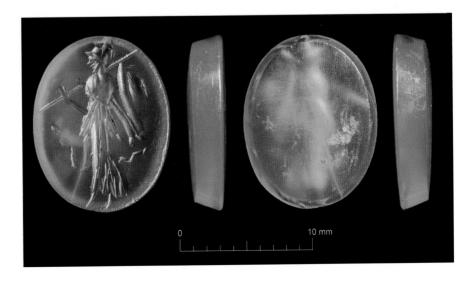

FIGURE 3.7 Gemstone of carnelian depicting the goddess Minerva, lost either by a Roman soldier or a Callevan around the time of the conquest

(PHOTO IAN R. CARTWRIGHT)

just proposed. While it is possible that Verica returned to Britain after the invasion as client king, ruling by Rome's permission, there is no record of this. However, we do know of a Cogidubnus (or Togidubnus), recorded on a greatly damaged inscription found at Chichester in 1723. According to a generally accepted reading of it, he styled himself as 'Great King in Britain'. This links with a comment by the Roman historian Tacitus that a King Cogidubnus was presented with certain 'civitates', perhaps best interpreted as tribal communities, occupying territories broadly equivalent to modern-day counties, and that he remained loyal down to his own times (the late 1st century AD). We do not know exactly when the award took place: it may have been in the late 40s in recognition of help given during the first revolt of the East Anglian Iceni in AD 47, or after the much more devastating Boudican rebellion of AD 60/61. Nor do we know the boundaries of Cogidubnus's kingdom in the first instance, except that it included Chichester, or the location of the 'certain tribal communities'. Assuming that for strategic reasons Calleva was not returned to either Verica or Cogidubnus in the years immediately following the invasion, either of those historical events could have provided the context for the transfer of ownership, that is, if the ownership of Calleva ever did transfer out of direct Roman control.

## Nero and Calleva

A complicating factor in trying to unravel the history of Calleva in the years following the Roman invasion and conquest of south-east Britain is that the first person of authority whom we can link with Calleva is Claudius's successor, the Emperor Nero (AD 54–68). Fragments of tiles stamped with his name and imperial titles have been found only at Calleva and at the brickworks where they were made at Little London, Pamber, 1.5 miles (2.4 km) south of the town (Fig. 3.8–3.9). The recent excavations have produced examples from across the town – from Insula IX in the north-west, through Insula III and the forum basilica in the centre of the town, to the temple enclosure in Insula XXX in the east, as well as from the brickworks and the original find from next to the baths in Insula XXXIII. It is hard to interpret the presence of these symbols of imperial authority, which have been found nowhere else in Britain, other than as evidence of imperial ownership of the town and a surrounding territory of unknown extent. But why might the Emperor show interest in this one particular town in the province? We can only speculate but, supposing Calleva was among the lands given to

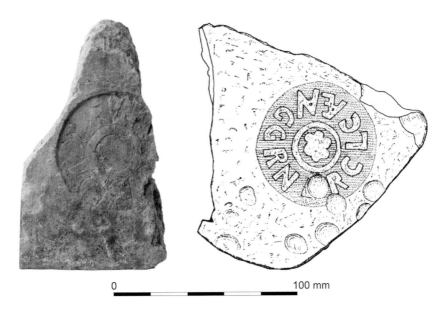

FIGURE 3.8 Nero tiles: the complete legend on the tile (right) reads Ner(o) Cl(audius) Cae(sar) Aug(ustus) Ger(manicus)

FIGURE 3.9 A tile kiln at Little London, Pamber, Hampshire, under excavation in 2017; aerial view of trench (right)

Cogidubnus, might he, in order to retain the support of the Emperor, have gifted them straight back? This would make sense if the return gift was made after the Boudican revolt, for this had been instigated by the annexation, on the authority of Catus Decianus, the procurator or financial administrator of the province, of the entire client kingdom of the Iceni, following the death of its king, Prasutagus. Cogidubnus may have hoped that, by returning the gift, in whole or in part, total annexation of his kingdom could be avoided, at least in his lifetime. Another explanation, which might fit better this unique association of the emperor with Calleva, bearing in mind that the annexation of the Icenian territory has not produced comparable evidence,

Combustion chamber

is that the town, with its excellent road connections (below, Chapter 5), was established as the temporary location of the headquarters of the provincial administration following Boudica's destruction of London. But why the imperial stamp? We know that Nero sent a senior member of his secretariat, the former slave Polyclitus, to undertake a commission of enquiry after the rebellion had been quelled. Acting on Nero's behalf, the use of the stamp in connection with whatever building or buildings were commissioned by Polyclitus to accommodate himself and his staff would indicate that the work had imperial sanction.

How then did Calleva fare under imperial ownership? The spread of the Nero tiles across the town implies a considerable building programme, perhaps a systematic attempt to turn the simple, one-room, wooden huts of the Iron Age settlement into a recognisably Roman town? The only Roman-style building that we know for certain that was built very soon after the conquest was the rectangular, timber-framed 'courtyard building' at the centre of the town and the only new streets that we can be reasonably certain of are the two that took traffic through the settlement east–west and north–south. While the presence of the tiles need not be taken as evidence of building with bricks and mortar, they do imply the construction of rectangular buildings requiring tiled roofs. As it happens, the great majority of the Nero-stamped tile is of tegulae, which, with the semicircular imbrex, make up the classic Roman roofing material which was designed to cover rectangular buildings. At this time, and across the province more widely, and in both military and civilian contexts, such buildings were almost exclusively built of timber. One notable exception, of course, is the bath house with its warm and hot rooms heated by great furnaces. Although examples of wooden construction are known, for the obvious reason of avoiding risk of fire, this type of structure was best built of masonry.

It might have been thought that when it came to re-build as timbers decayed, especially perhaps in the case of public buildings, the opportunity would be taken to replace in masonry rather than timber. However, when it was only about 10–15 years old, and after possible destruction by fire, the 'courtyard building' in the centre of the town was re-built in wood, probably in the AD 60s, also the preferred material of the building which eventually replaced it (Chapter 4).

Not surprising, perhaps, the first building of masonry construction which we know of at Calleva is the bath house. First uncovered in 1903–4 during the Society of Antiquaries' campaign, it was observed that the building did not align with the Roman street grid, suggesting that it pre-dated it. As we shall

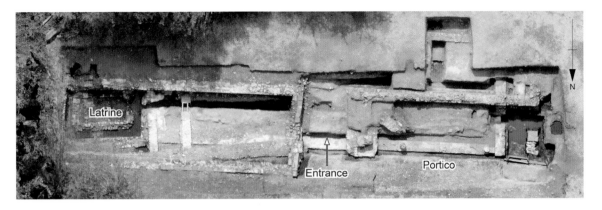

FIGURE 3.10 Aerial view of the entrance, portico and latrine of the public baths in 2018

see in the next chapter the evidence points to a date late in the 1st century AD for a regular system of streets across the town, so the baths ought to be earlier than that. The discovery in the cess pit next to the latrines of a stray Nero tile, the only one to be found in the town till 1977, strengthened the case for building during his reign. Fresh excavation of the baths, 2018–19 and ongoing at the time of writing, has added further evidence for a Neronian date, probably between the mid-50s and the mid-60s. The structure was an imposing one, built of regularly squared, Wealden Greensand blocks with interleaving brick courses – the brick matching that made at Little London – and with a portico supported by finely turned, dwarf columns of a Gloucestershire limestone (Fig. 3.10). The portico led into an open courtyard or exercise area beyond which were the baths proper with their suite of changing, warm and hot rooms, and cold pool. Alongside the baths was the ditch of the Iron Age Inner Earthwork which was cleaned out to act as the drain from the baths' latrine. Right from the bottom and the start of the use of the baths the silts contained quantities of the eggs of human intestinal parasites such as whipworm – clearly the inhabitants of Calleva were not always in the best of health! A richer story of the development of these baths is only now becoming clear from both the environmental evidence and, as the re-excavation shows us clearly, the plan, first published in 1905, which is essentially that of a later, new build of a substantially larger bath house dating to around the turn of the 1st and 2nd centuries.

## Elsewhere in Calleva

What we know of other buildings of the Neronian town is that timber and almost exclusively oak was the preferred material, even for public buildings.

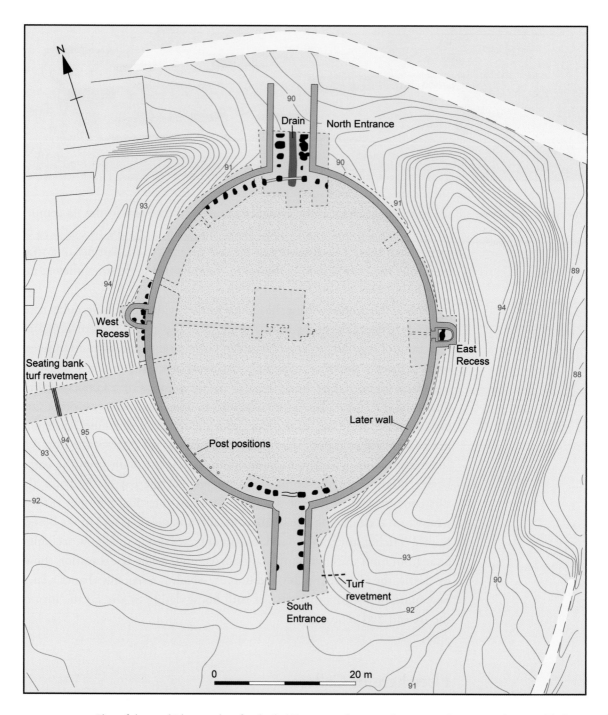

N

90

Drain    North Entrance

91

90

93

91

94

89

West
Recess

East
Recess

94

Seating bank
turf revetment

88

Later wall

95

94  95

Post positions

93

92

93

90

92

Turf
revetment

92

South
Entrance

0                        20 m

91

FIGURE 3.11 Plan of the amphitheatre when first built AD 55–65 with its circular arena and entrances shown in black

We see this with the amphitheatre which was built at the eastern edge of the settlement with its two entrances aligned on the Iron Age, north-east to south-west orientation (Fig. 3.11). Unusually, and uniquely in Britain, it had a circular, rather than an elliptical arena, about 43 m in diameter, which was enclosed by a timber revetment and entered through the two opposing entrances (Fig. 3.12). The seating banks, which stand about 6.5 m above the arena (about 3.5 m above the original ground surface), were made up of dumps of the gravel and clay excavated to create the arena. Traces of terracing around the inner face of the bank may have supported seating. If so, the capacity of the amphitheatre was about 3500. Otherwise the terraces could have accommodated over 7000 standing spectators (two figures which may give clues as to the minimal and maximal population of the town in the later 1st century AD).

We have no idea as to how the amphitheatre was used, but we can reasonably assume that it hosted a mix of animal and gladiatorial contests although, because the arena is circular, we might infer that riding displays also took place. The only other circular arena that we know of in Britain at this time is the gyrus (a circular fenced enclosure) at the Roman fort at Baginton, near Coventry, which is thought to have been used for training horses. Although the animal bone was very poorly preserved, some evidence

FIGURE 3.12 Excavation of the north (left) entrance and across the south (right) entrance of the amphitheatre showing the excavated pits for the posts which revetted the entrance passages and arena of the first phase AD 55–65

in support of equestrian use of the arena is provided by finds of horse bone, which, compared with domestic contexts within the town, was more abundant than the usually ubiquitous cattle, sheep and pig. Among the remains are those of a horse skull deliberately placed, presumably as a votive offering, at the base of one of the post pits of the initial construction. Other animals which might have appeared in the arena include bulls and brown bear. The Roman poet Martial tells of the appearance of a Caledonian bear in the arena in Rome in the reign of the Emperor Domitian (AD 81–96).

Where public or potentially palatial buildings in 1st century Calleva are concerned, there remains a mystery: built into the foundations of the timber town house, which was constructed in Insula IX between the late 1st and mid-2nd centuries, were pieces of architectural stonework, including column fragments, of Bath stone, clearly derived from a demolished building of some considerable grandeur within the town (Fig. 3.13). The accounts by the Society of Antiquaries' excavators also mention occasional finds of similar pieces of stone from the central insulae of the town. We can only surmise that the building was part of the Neronian project but what was it and where was it located? Geophysical survey has so far failed to find a possible candidate for investigation but if the building (or buildings?) in question was thoroughly demolished and its site subsequently built over, it would be hard to detect.

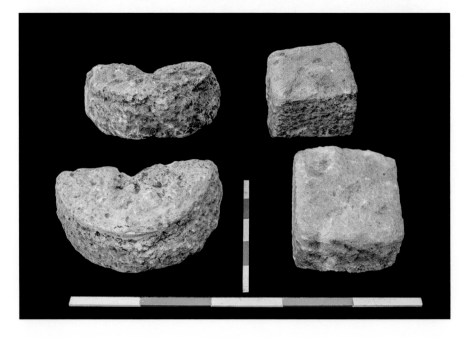

FIGURE 3.13 Architectural fragments of Bath limestone robbed from a grand 1st century Roman building in Calleva and incorporated in the foundations of the late 1st/early 2nd century town house in Insula IX. The scales are 0.5 m and 1.0 m

# Over in Insula IX

What of the rest of the town in the first three to four decades following the Roman invasion, a time in which a whole generation would have grown up not knowing of life before the conquest? Our most substantial evidence comes from Insula IX, the only part of the town where there has been a large area excavated down to reveal the late Iron Age and early Roman settlement. As we saw in Chapter 2, in its earliest phase, before the Roman conquest, the area was dominated by a large timber hall aligned north-east to south-west situated within a compound edged by trackways on two sides, one similarly oriented, the other north-west to south-east. These trackways continued to be used alongside the new, axial, Roman north–south street, which provided the eastern boundary of the compound and began to influence development within it.

Shortly after the conquest, the great hall was demolished and replaced on the same footprint by a shorter version which respected the course of the new north–south street. Otherwise the excavated space was occupied by a mix of small, circular and rectangular buildings, their foundations defined by spreads of yellow clay (Fig. 3.14). While the same sorts of building may have occupied the space around the great hall of the pre-conquest occupation, it was the use of clay to floor these early buildings which made them recognisable and defined their footprints. By the AD 70s and 80s it was single-story rectangular buildings which fronted the north–south highway, while the space between them and the bounding trackways was mostly occupied by roundhouses (Fig. 3.15). These were small, single cell structures with a central hearth. Setting aside the hall building with its floor area of 280 m², the internal area of the best-preserved rectangular building was 72 m² (the average floor area of a modern terrace house is about 32 m²). By comparison the largest roundhouse had a floor area of 40–50 m², the smallest, a mere 10–15 m². These would have been of wattle-type construction, so needed only relatively simple materials.

That the Iron Age north-east to south-west alignment survived to this period can be seen in the orientation of both the smaller hall and a partly revealed building at the southern limit of the excavated area. On the other hand, both the rectangular buildings, which fronted on to the street, were aligned with it, the better preserved of the two more clearly so than the other. It contained a succession of hearths and adjacent to it, on the south side, were sub-rectangular pits which might initially have served as wells but were ultimately used for human cess, as indicated by the presence

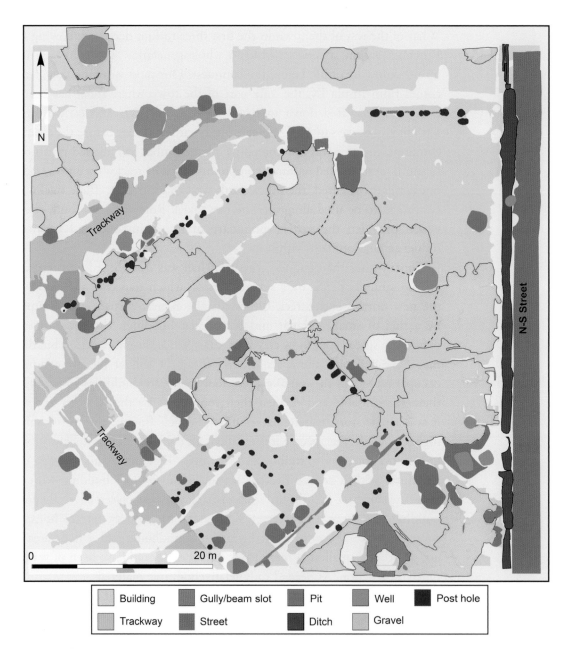

FIGURE 3.14  Plan of the excavated area in Insula IX between the mid-40s and the mid-80s of the 1st century AD. It shows the remains of the post-holes of the successor to the late Iron Age hall, the clay floors of the round and rectangular buildings, the two trackways, the wells and rubbish pits. Compare with Fig. 3.15

FIGURE 3.15
Reconstruction of
Insula IX about AD
80, looking across the
north-south street
towards the north-west
(by Margaret Mathews).
Compare with Fig. 3.14

of abundant mineralised food remains. Water was then obtained from a shallow, 2.7 m deep well which had been lined with a barrel made of silver fir, a species whose natural habitat is not to be found in Britain but in mountainous regions such as the Alps or Pyrenees. It is likely, therefore, that this barrel, like others found in the town by the early excavators, originally carried wine.

The position of this building next to the street and a group of pits containing abundant food remains suggests that it was a small taberna, providing food and drink to travellers passing through the town. Among the buildings and rubbish pits to the rear of the taberna, finds of spindle whorls and needles indicate spinning, weaving and sewing of woollen clothing, while the presence of awls, small iron punches along with the needles suggests leather-working as well.

Other finds from rubbish pits associated with the occupation of this area give insight into the standard of living. While finds of metalwork are relatively rare compared with the large quantities of pottery, the collection of copper alloy artefacts is dominated by brooches, followed by toilet instruments, consisting of tweezers, nail-cleaners and ear-picks (Fig. 3.16). While some of these items were imported into the town, such as a brooch type found more commonly north of the Thames and in Colchester, others were probably made (and repaired) locally. One remarkable find dating to this period is the leaded bronze foot topped by a figure of the Egyptian deity Harpocrates from a Campanian wine-warmer or brazier such as have been found in Pompeii, Italy (Fig. 3.17). Many hobnails from footwear were found, and perhaps some were from leather shoes and boots made in this part of the town, but the ironwork is dominated by fittings associated with construction, especially nails. These are not particularly large and may have come from wooden furniture or vehicles as well as from buildings, where they may have been used to fasten planks to the frames of the rectangular buildings fronting on to the north–south street.

0     10 mm

FIGURE 3.16  A set of copper-alloy toilet instruments: tweezers, nail cleaner and ear scoop

0     1     2 cm

FIGURE 3.17  The bronze foot of a Campanian wine-warmer or brazier in the form of the Egyptian deity Harpocrates from Insula IX: front, side and rear views

## The Silchester Eagle

One of the most celebrated finds from Silchester which dates to this period is the bronze eagle which was found by Joyce in his excavation of the forum basilica in 1866 (Figs 1.7, 3.18). Examination of his diaries suggests it was buried in the foundations of the building in the early 2nd century. Despite the loss of its wings it is still an exceptionally fine piece, consistent with comparable work made at the start of the Roman imperial period. It has been described as 'the most superbly naturalistic rendering of any bird or beast so far yielded by Roman Britain'. It was originally probably part of a larger statue group, either of an emperor or of Jupiter, the eagle at the feet looking up.

## Eating and drinking in Insula IX

The pottery includes a wide range of imported tableware, mostly beakers, cups and platters, and, for the most part, from the same workshops in northern France which had supplied the Iron Age community. Although imported in small quantities before AD 43, the red glossy samian tableware manufactured at La Graufesenque, near Toulouse in southern France became a regular and distinctive presence in the post-conquest rubbish deposits (Fig. 3.19). Cooking and storage vessels were locally made. Although wheel-thrown vessels made in kilns located some 15 miles (25 km) distant in Alice Holt Forest, near Farnham, Surrey become a regular feature of the discarded pottery of this period (below, Fig. 3.22), the latter continued to

FIGURE 3.20 A cooking
pot of late Iron Age
and earliest Roman
handmade, flint-
tempered Silchester
Ware

be dominated by the local, bonfire-fired, handmade, Iron Age-style, flint-tempered 'Silchester Ware' (Fig. 3.20). There was also a brief period of pottery production alongside brick-making at Little London, where three kilns firing a range of 'Roman-style' wheel-thrown vessels including flagons and mortaria were excavated in 2017.

Food remains which, for the first time at Calleva, include human waste in the form of mineralised seed and plant remains, indicate a broader diet than in the late Iron Age. As well as the consumption of beef, lamb, mutton and pork, the main sources of meat, that of wild species including red and roe deer and hare were also eaten. Domestic fowl was also consistently present in rubbish deposits and other birds such as duck, woodcock and thrush were also consumed. The cess pits next to the taberna also produced an abundance of common eel, but also freshwater fish such as salmon, trout, pike, roach, chub and mullet. Fish bone is best preserved in mineralised contexts and its absence in the Iron Age may only be a reflection of the lack of such deposits, but it may also be the case that fish and eel were only added to the diet of the Callevans after the conquest.

Although spelt wheat and hulled barley remained the main staples as far as plant food is concerned, other cultivated species, notably flax, pea and bean are also represented. Flax is usually viewed as a textile crop, but charred seeds associated with domestic hearths suggest it may have also been consumed as a food. The people of Insula IX also ate a rich variety of other plant foods, many of which were imported, including exotics such as caraway, fig, fennel, lentils and mulberry, all of which were probably never cultivated in Roman Britain, but also apple/pear, cherry, bullace, celery, coriander, grape and plum which were also eaten in the decades immediately following the conquest. While some of the latter may have been imported at first, they were subsequently cultivated here. Wild fruits including blackberry, elderberry and sloe were also consumed and hazel nutshell was frequently represented.

We now have the individual components which made up the diet of these early Callevans, but how were they consumed? Our ability to analyse and identify the lipid residues trapped on the inside of pottery cooking vessels gives us a clue. Essentially the analysis reveals a continuity of practice from the pre-conquest period; the pottery vessels were used for cooking all the main types of meat represented by the animal bones found on the site as well as fish. And, as in the late Iron Age, there was a general lack of milk or dairy fats.

Although some types of food, such as the imports, were rarer than locally grown or wild species, all of them were available across the Insula IX neighbourhood suggesting a degree of affluence with no apparent distinction in consumption between the occupants of round and rectangular houses, both of modest character. However, if we look across to the forum basilica site and the 'courtyard building' barely more than 100 metres away to the south-east, there are some notable differences, though the absence of deposits containing waterlogged or mineralised remains makes it impossible to compare the types of plant foods consumed. What is striking is the abundance of marine shellfish, mainly oyster, and some mussel, but remarkably few of them from the Insula IX neighbourhood (see also below, p. 74). While this may simply reflect different dietary preferences, it is more likely that the occupants of the 'courtyard building' were more affluent than their neighbours to the north-west. In his *Natural History*, written sometime in the AD 70s, Pliny the Elder tells us that British oysters were exported to Rome and this in itself suggests that they were a fairly expensive foodstuff at this period, especially in inland Silchester. Added weight to the idea that the people living in the 'courtyard building' were quite affluent is given by the presence there of a greater number and variety of imported amphorae compared with the small assemblage of identifiable vessels from Insula IX. At the 'courtyard building', besides a preponderance of olive-oil carrying vessels from southern Spain, we find wine-carrying amphoras from north-east and southern Spain, Italy, the Aegean and southern France, small, carrot-shaped vessels containing dried fruits from Palestine and vessels carrying the fish sauce known as garum, while at Insula IX there are mainly just olive oil-carrying amphoras from southern Spain and wine amphoras from southern France, with just a very few sherds of Italian (Campanian) wine amphoras. A further potential wealth distinction between the two areas can be found in the greater incidence – by a factor of three – of coins found in contemporary deposits at the basilica site compared with Insula IX. Clearly, there was greater spending power at the centre compared with the more peripheral neighbourhood and this would be consistent with Roman officials occupying the building.

## The Roman town takes shape

With the provision of civic baths, an amphitheatre and the spread of numerous domestic and commercial buildings with their distinctive red-tiled roofs across the town, the Nero project had begun to transform the Iron Age settlement into a recognisably Roman town, one which might begin to bear comparison with the first Roman colony of the province, founded at Colchester on the site of the legionary fortress in AD 49 (Fig. 3.21). This is only what we know so far, but our sample is tiny, given that only about 0.5 hectares, barely 1%, of the early Roman town has been investigated. Were there other public buildings in the town at this time, such as a theatre to complement the amphitheatre, or temples, or even a circus? Were there bath houses or hypocausts associated with any private buildings? An obvious area to investigate the beginning of temple building is Insula VII, to the south of the central insula containing the 'courtyard building', where the masonry-built polygonal temple discovered by Joyce may well have had a predecessor.

Beyond the defensive enclosure of the Inner Earthwork to the east the ground rises up from the stream below and some of this higher ground was occupied by what later became a sacred enclosure containing three temples (Insula XXX). The excavation of one of these in 2017 produced traces of a possible timber predecessor which was roofed with tiles bearing the Neronian stamp (see Fig. 3.8). Such was the significance of this building that a large quantity of its roofing tile was carefully buried in a pit dug in

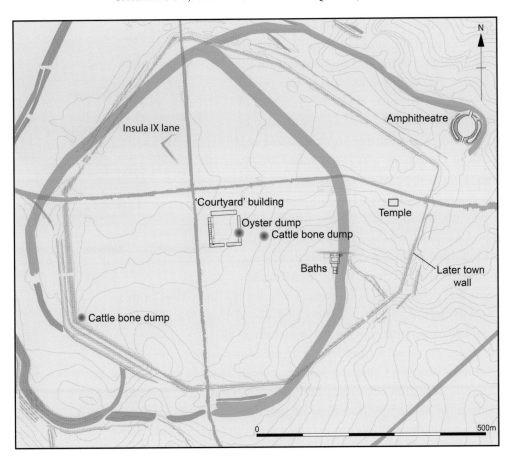

FIGURE 3.21 Calleva in the time of Nero

what became the central shrine of its later, masonry successor. Clearly, much more of the early town awaits discovery and it would be good to resolve the mystery of the building (or buildings) which incorporated monumental masonry in its or their construction.

One obvious difference between Neronian Calleva and the colony of Camulodunum at Colchester is the lack of a regular street grid, despite there being at least two main streets which cut across the town and over-rode the lanes of Iron Age Calleva. We have noted how those lanes in Insula IX continued to be used in the Neronian town and how the orientations of the amphitheatre and baths also follow the Iron Age arrangement. We can only speculate why the opportunity was not taken to lay out a regular grid when so much else was changing in the town, one possible reason being that, to do so, would have involved both the destruction of all the buildings which lay in the paths of the new streets and the associated redefinition of property boundaries.

Another dimension of town life which reflects on how it was managed at this time concerns the disposal of rubbish. Besides noting the numerous rubbish pits which were dug in Insula IX, it is to this period that the dense mass of waste from the butchery of cattle was deposited towards the south-west edge of the settlement. Also attributable to this period is a huge deposit of cattle bone which was found by the Antiquaries' just to the east of the forum in Insula VI and an extensive and deep spread of oyster shell close by beneath the east side of the forum, both middens perhaps to be associated with the life of the 'courtyard building' (above, p. 71). Rubbish was also being dumped in the ditch of the now redundant Inner Earthwork defence. With noisome waste being disposed of both in the heart of, as well as on the periphery of Calleva, there was clearly no over-arching urban authority controlling waste disposal.

FIGURE 3.22 Mid–late 1st century Alice Holt jar

Overall, there was, then, a considerable degree of continuity in the life of the inhabitants of Iron Age Calleva in the first 40 years or so after the Roman invasion. To the excavator, the most visible sign of this was the continued and ubiquitous use of the very Iron Age looking, flint-tempered, handmade pottery used for cooking and storage. Locally made, though we do not know exactly where, this accounts for up to two-thirds (by weight) of the pottery from the Insula IX neighbourhood. But there are also the beginnings of change among which may be noted the appearance of wheel-thrown, grey ware pottery, notably that from Alice Holt Forest (above, p. 69) (Fig. 3.22). This accounts for about 10% of all the pottery and was used for cooking, serving and storage. There was also an increase in the number of iron nails and the quantity of brick and tile from the site. Nails were almost completely absent before the conquest, but about 1300 were found in deposits of this time, along with some 200 kg of brick and tile.

Perhaps the changes with the greatest impact resulted from the increased demands for building materials, not only timber, but also the ironmongery and specialised tools and, of course, the skilled craftsmen, such as blacksmiths, to make the tools and carpenters to erect the new Roman-style buildings where oak was very much the preferred material. To give an indication of the scale of demand for resources, it has been estimated, for example, that the construction of the amphitheatre alone required the felling of over 27 hectares (68 acres) of natural woodland. If the areas of the town where we have glimpsed the occupation of these first Roman decades are representative, then the great majority of buildings within the town were new build in this period. At the same the local woodland would also be looked to as a source of fuel, not only for the requirements of the domestic household, but also the new demands, such as firing the brick and pottery kilns at Little London, heating the public baths, firing the blacksmiths' forges and fuelling the food outlets set up to meet the demands of passing traffic.

We should also not forget the new fashion of equipping our simple round and rectangular buildings with clay floors. The clay had to be dug from pits outside the town and carted in. The demand for iron to provide the tools and ironmongery – nails, joiner's dogs and other fastenings and fittings – would also have increased. No wonder that the transition from round to rectangular (if that was peoples' preference) could only have been a gradual one; roundhouses of wattle construction needed hardly any carpentered timbers or ironmongery.

In concluding this Chapter we should take a bird's eye view and try and imagine how the town would have looked in the early 80s, 40 years on from the invasion. We might see a township, still pretty much confined within the remains of the great defensive circuit of the Inner Earthwork, its rampart slighted and its ditch largely filled, but occupied with a mix of rectangular buildings with roofs of either thatch or red tile and roundhouses roofed with either thatch or turf. Like the hall in Insula IX, some of the buildings would have been much larger than their immediate neighbours, anticipating, perhaps, the distribution of the town houses which characterised the 2nd–4th century town. The straight lines of the two main streets might be distinguished by the (mostly?) tile-roofed buildings which fronted on to them, perhaps more densely clustered along the east–west than the north–south street for the former carried the busiest traffic between London and the west country. Otherwise, with its network of lanes on the north-east to south-west/north-west to south-east alignment, the town might not have looked so very different from its late Iron Age predecessor.

# CHAPTER FOUR

# From town to city:
# Calleva, a regional centre

........................................................................................................

After the death of Nero, it was some 15 years or so before significant new developments took place at Calleva. The greatest of these was the laying out of the regular street grid which is such a distinctive feature of the town (Fig. 4.1). Making it would have involved destroying the properties which lay in its path – the surface area of all the new streets together the equivalent of about 2 hectares: 2 hectares of a thriving town. The laying down of the grid must have raised questions about the ownership of the existing compounds which had to be divided or truncated by the new streets.

The orientation of the grid followed that of the north–south and east–west streets laid out in the later 40s onwards when communication and movement of supplies between London and the garrisons to the west became vital to the advance of the frontier and the security of the province. The making of the streets was an enormous undertaking involving the quarrying of tonnes of gravel from extensive deposits to the west and carting it into the town. The streets were initially about 7 m wide and 0.3–0.5 m high at the crest, sloping down to drainage ditches on either side. This is impressive enough but traffic on the main streets was so heavy that successive re-surfacings eventually took the height of the north–south street to at least 1 m above the original ground surface and almost certainly higher in the case of the much busier east–west street.

The street grid is extremely well preserved, making it one of the hallmarks of the Roman town. Analysis of its plan reveals actual measurements which closely correspond to three recurring dimensions of 250, 275 and 400 Roman feet with the streets measuring 25 Roman feet in width (a Roman foot =

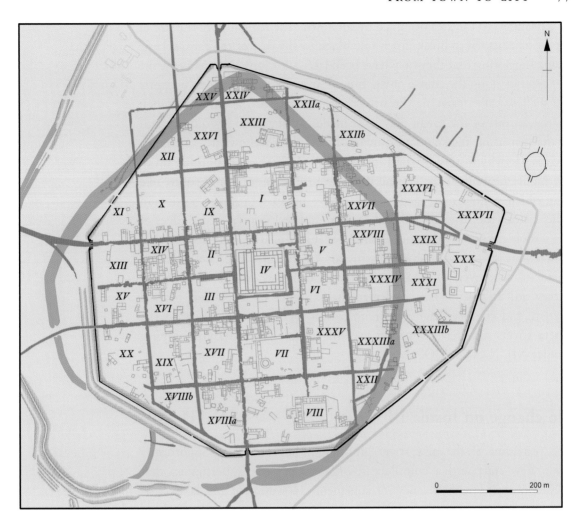

FIGURE 4.1 Plan of the Roman street grid of Calleva. It partly overlies the course of the late Iron Age Inner Earthwork

0.971 ft or 29.6 cm). This regularity of the grid suggests that most of the streets were completed as a single operation. The insulae either side of the central insula which contained the post-conquest 'courtyard building' were further divided by an east–west street. This deviates slightly to the south as it heads east from the central insula across the now infilled Inner Earthwork to what may have been already, but certainly soon became, the trapezoidal temple enclosure at the eastern edge of the town (Insula XXX). The creation of this cul-de-sac meant that the next street to the north became the main east–west thoroughfare of the town. Its course takes it around the northern edge of the temple enclosure to meet the road from London.

It is only on the eastern side that the street grid extends across and beyond the course of the Inner Earthwork, adding about 20 acres (*c.* 8 hectares) to the area occupied by the town. The regularity of the size of the insulae begins to break down one block to the east of the central large insula suggesting that they may have been later additions. Alternatively, the wet ground along the course of the Inner Earthwork ditch, which occupies the shallow valley carrying the stream past the site of the baths and then south-east out of the town, may have made it difficult to lay out the grid to the east using the standard dimensions employed elsewhere. Certainly, the insulae which straddle the Inner Earthwork ditch and continue up to the higher ground to the east all differ from one another and some, like that which contains the public baths, have no eastern street border. In other places, too, the regularity of the system breaks down at the edges of the settlement and we cannot be certain that any of the peripheral insulae, which were truncated by the construction of the later 2nd century town defences, were ever finished as complete rectangles. Neither geophysical survey nor excavation has confirmed the existence of any streets beyond the late 2nd century defensive circuit except, perhaps, to the north-west, where streets may have extended over the Inner Earthwork to complete Insulae XII, XXV and XXVI.

## No change on Insula IX

The provision of the new street grid might have been an opportunity for a new start and a complete re-organisation of properties so that they conformed with the new arrangement. However, in Insula IX that opportunity was not taken and the western boundaries of the Central Compound which had contained the late Iron Age hall and its mid-1st century successor remained unchanged until the late 3rd century. Likewise, the orientation of the new buildings within the excavated area perpetuated that of its predecessors in the late Iron Age (Fig. 4.2). Indeed, the north-east to south-west alignment of the new group of residential buildings, arguably the successors of the earlier halls, corresponds very closely with sunrise at the mid-summer solstice and sunset at the mid-winter solstice. This was also the case with the group of small dwellings immediately to the south, including the successor to the earlier taberna, which was built over it and met the north–south street at an angle of 45°. The awkwardness of this arrangement emphasises the importance to the occupants of re-asserting a tradition with possible cosmological significance over the convenience of a neat alignment with the street.

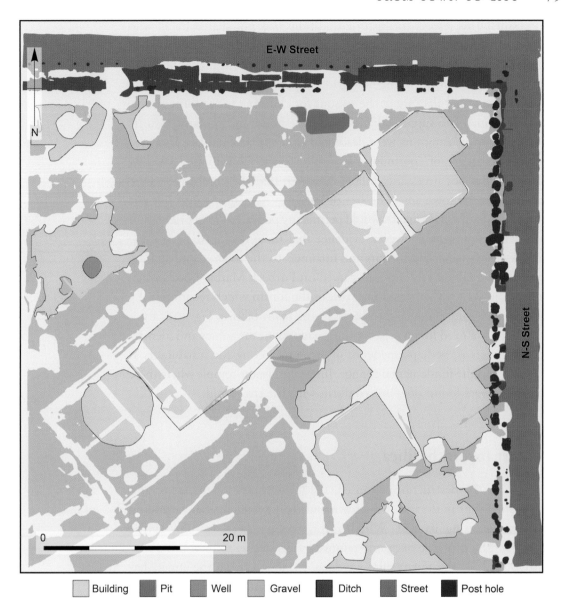

E-W Street

N

N-S Street

0                 20 m

| Building | Pit | Well | Gravel | Ditch | Street | Post hole |

FIGURE 4.2
Major change: plan of
the excavated area of
Insula IX after the laying
out of the street grid in
the late 1st century AD.
The buildings – all of
timber (ERTB I–II) –
still follow the late Iron
Age alignment

A number of buildings across the town plan share orientations which
are quite at variance with the grain of the street grid and this has led to
speculation about an early Roman town plan. We now know that these
various orientations relate back to the Iron Age layout of Calleva and that,
just as with the retention of the historic property boundaries mentioned
above, buildings like those in Insula IX, which do not conform with the
Roman street grid, are deliberate re-assertions of the orientation of their

predecessors. This respect for historic traditions was not shared by all who built anew in the late 1st and early 2nd centuries and there are insulae, such as the central group of I, IV and VII, where there is no hint of a building which does not conform to the new grid.

We can only speculate about the reasons for choosing to conform or not, but it is reasonable to suppose that those whose houses perpetuated historic alignments and orientations were descendants of the original late Iron Age occupants, evidence of continuous ownership since the founding years of Calleva. It does not necessarily follow, however, that the conformists were newcomers to the town since the size of late Iron Age compounds like the Central Compound in Insula IX would permit any permutation of orientation of a building within it. However, evidence that there may have been some kind of split between old residents and incomers to the town is hinted at by a group of fragmentary inscriptions carved on Purbeck Marble from a small temple in Insula XXXV to the south-east of the forum which record gifts by a guild of peregrini, literally 'foreigners' in the town (above, Figs 1.10, 1.12). That there was a need for an organisation to represent the values and identity of the incomers is, perhaps, evidence of tensions among the inhabitants at this period of quite fundamental change. Interestingly, the temple where these inscriptions were found does not conform with the street grid.

## The first forum basilica

Not least for the destruction it caused, the laying down of the street grid was a major event in the life of the town and clear evidence of a controlling authority exercising its will. Whether this was a direct decision of the governor of the province or at one remove by his decree to establish a new ordo (council) of the town's elite we do not know. Dating the streets has proved difficult but the best and most extensive evidence comes from Insula IX which points to a date around AD 85. This coincides with the date of another major development in the town, the provision of a forum basilica, a building which combines the functions of civic and judicial administration (basilica) with a market place (forum) (Fig. 4.3).

The forum basilica, occupying the central block of the town, had been explored both by the Reverend Joyce and the Antiquaries in the 19th century. As we have seen, the excavations of the 1980s focused on the hall, the basilica which flanked the west side of the complex and the occupation which lay beneath it. In the previous chapter we described the 'courtyard

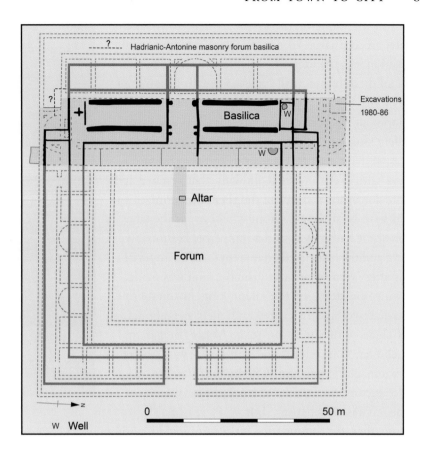

FIGURE 4.3 A conjectural plan of the late 1st century AD timber forum basilica

building' built in the late AD 40s. Above this building, but beneath the material used to make up the floor of the masonry basilica, found by the antiquarians, were the remains of another great timber building. This had been constructed with deep foundation trenches to accommodate the massive sleeper beams necessary to support the columns which flanked the nave, the latter bisected by an entrance hall (Fig. 4.4). This led through to the central room, probably a shrine, of a western range. A small trench dug opposite it and just to the east of the entrance into the forum revealed a masonry altar base, where dedications could be made by those entering the basilica. While there has been considerable debate about the purpose of the earlier 'courtyard building', the hall-like character of the later structure clearly looks forward, anticipating its masonry replacement and can be identified as a timber basilica, the new seat of justice.

The construction of this building is taken to represent a very significant development in the governance of the town and the surrounding countryside. The forum basilica is associated with the setting up of the structure of the administrative unit of the civitas, where town and country are seen as one administrative unit for purposes of taxation and the exercise of justice, in this case the civitas of the Atrebates with Calleva formally becoming Calleva Atrebatum, the city of the Atrebates. This development has been associated with the break-up of the client kingdom following the death of Cogidubnus, but, as we have seen in Chapter 3, the association of Calleva with Nero makes it unlikely that, even if it had previously formed part of the client kingdom, this would have been the case from whenever in the later 50s or 60s it had passed to that emperor. Presumably Calleva and the associated estate remained in imperial hands after Nero's death until the decision was made, following the death of the client king, to establish the civitates of the Atrebates and their neighbours, the Belgae with their centre at Venta Belgarum (Winchester, Hampshire) and the Regni with theirs at Noviomagus Regnorum (Chichester, West Sussex).

No documents survive which indicate the extent of the civitas Atrebatum, but it is reasonable to suppose that the boundaries either coincided with major geographical features like the River Thames or that they fell midway between Calleva and its neighbouring civitas capitals of Cirencester, Winchester and Chichester, or major towns like London and Verulamium (St Albans) (Fig. 4.5). Along the roads radiating from the town the boundary of the civitas probably coincided with significant intermediate settlements, some of which can be identified with Roman-named places: Cunetio (Mildenhall, Wiltshire) to the west, Durocornovium (Wanborough, Wiltshire) to the north-west, Dorchester-on-Thames (Oxfordshire) to the north, Pontes (Staines, Surrey) to the east, Onna (Neatham, Hampshire) to the south-east, and Leucomagus (East Anton, Hampshire) to the south-west. No road between Calleva and Verulamium has so far been convincingly identified, so here the Thames is likely to have formed part of the north and eastern boundary of the civitas. The territory thus defined includes the historic, pre-1974 county of Berkshire: the middle stretch of the Thames Valley, the chalklands of the Berkshire Downs to the north of the town and the Hampshire Downs to the south.

Given the date of the timber forum basilica and the establishment of the

FIGURE 4.4 Deep foundation trench containing the remains of the oak sleeper beam which supported the aisle posts of the late 1st century forum basilica

contemporary street grid, the new administrative arrangement took place about AD 85. Since there are no further references of any kind of imperial ownership at Calleva, we can speculate that the founding of the civitas was prompted, if not facilitated, by the sale of the imperial estate. The funds raised could have contributed to the costs of setting up the civitas, including the buildings and street grid thought by the authorities to be appropriate for its chief town. Funds did not, however, stretch to building the forum basilica in masonry! A date around the mid-80s also corresponds more-or-less with the end of the governorship of Britannia by Agricola, who, thanks to the eulogistic biography written by his father-in-law, the great Roman historian Tacitus, is credited with encouraging the development of those parts of the province which had been released from military control.

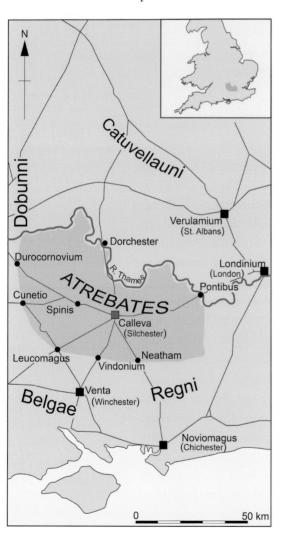

FIGURE 4.5 Map of the civitas of the Atrebates

If the town had self-governing status from the late 1st century onwards, we would expect it to have been run by councillors (decurions) drawn from suitably wealthy property owners in the town. We do not have any inscriptions which might shed light on this, only the existence of the forum basilica, which we associate with the running of town and civitas, the great hall of the basilica being the setting for the administration of justice. However, some of the finds from the occupation of the timber basilica suggest the possibility of a different arrangement. Surprisingly, more than half of the higher status finds, those of copper alloy other than brooches, are of pieces, mostly fragments, of military equipment which suggest a continuing, though not necessarily exclusive role for the military in the running of the town (Fig. 4.6).

A further strand of evidence which links the military with activity in the town at this time is the occurrence of brick and tile marked on the edge with tally marks, mostly simple crosses, or combinations of crosses and vertical or sloping lines. Although the basilica was built of timber, the entrance hall was partly paved with ceramic tile which had these markings. It would also have been roofed with tile, but none of this, of course, survived *in situ*. Why connect these simple markings with the military? The site where they have previously been reported in some quantity is also in southern Britain, the bath house associated with the British fleet, the *Classis Britannica*, at Beauport Park in East Sussex, as well as at other military sites, including others connected with the fleet. While it might not be surprising for military architects and engineers to be involved in the construction of a major building like the forum basilica, we would not ordinarily expect evidence of their continued presence to be found in the layers associated with the life of the building. If we consider how much tile would have been needed to roof the whole of the timber basilica and its associated forum at this time, then the construction and firing of new tile kilns specially dedicated for this purpose would not be surprising.

0    1    2 cm

FIGURE 4.6 Copper alloy razor handle from the late 1st century AD forum basilica. Note the zoomorphic terminal

## The baths

Similarly marked brick and tile has also been found at the site of the public bath house in the south-east quarter of the town. The public bath house is another major building that we can also associate with this stage in Calleva's development (Figs 4.7–4.8). Nero's bath house can only have been about 25–30 years old when it was demolished and replaced on the same footprint by a considerably larger facility. What prompted this is unclear, though one possibility is that the original building suffered from flooding as it was in the lowest part of the town, close to the springs that supplied its water. The new bath house also had to be near the springs, so to avoid floods the new floor level was raised by about half a metre. While bricks and tiles with tally marks identical to those found at the forum basilica have so far only been found re-used in later phases of the bath house or in the loose debris from its ultimate demolition, it is to be expected that military architects and engineers would have designed and overseen the building of such a complicated building. Unlike the forum basilica, to reduce the risk of fire it was built of masonry and, while some of the material used in the Neronian building such as the distinctive blocks of Wealden Greensand could have been re-cycled, new materials, including all the tile needed to roof it, would certainly have been required. In addition to the distinctive tally marks mentioned above, such

FIGURE 4.7 Plan of the early 2nd century bath house

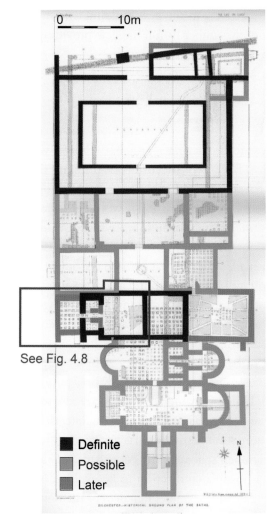

See Fig. 4.8

Definite
Possible
Later

FIGURE 4.8 Tepidarium (warm room) of the early 2nd century public bath house highlighted

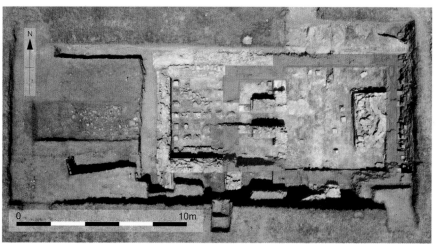

brick that has survived *in situ* in the new building is in the same distinctive red fabric as that from the timber forum basilica, providing further evidence of a new phase of brick and tile manufacture.

## A mansio

Constructing a new forum basilica and bath house would have taken considerable resources but, if we are correct in thinking that the 'courtyard building' beneath it was to support traffic passing through the town on official business, then a replacement for it would also have been required. There is one other major public building which we know of from the antiquarian excavations which might well have met this need. This is the large building in Insula VIII near what became the South Gate of the town. Consisting of three ranges of rooms around a courtyard, and with a footprint of 3900 m², this was the second largest building in the town of any date (Fig. 4.9). It is also the only building in the town other than the public baths which was equipped with its own bath house. It is generally regarded as a mansio, a building to be used by officials and other travellers on imperial business and needing to make use of the cursus publicus, the imperial posting service. This building would certainly repay renewed excavation, not least to discover whether it was first built in the late 1st century. It would also give an opportunity to investigate parts not previously explored, such as the large, apparently open spaces of the courtyard and the adjacent walled yard. There is also a possible connection to be explored with a completely unexcavated building outside the later defences of the town. Between it and the mansio, when the defences were first constructed towards the end of the 2nd century, provision was allowed for a postern gate, a very rare occurrence in the town's defences. This gate could have enabled individuals, on foot or on horseback, but not vehicles, to move between the two buildings.

The scale of the building with its provision of a dedicated bath house, the division of the wings into suites, with heated reception rooms in the west range, are all consistent with the interpretation as a mansio. Buildings of a similar plan and scale have been found elsewhere in Britain, not surprisingly also in the smaller settlements along the major roads between the larger towns, for example at Wanborough on the road from Silchester to Cirencester and at Godmanchester on the road from London to Lincoln and the north. Similar buildings are also to be found on the continent, as at the town of Kempten in southern Germany.

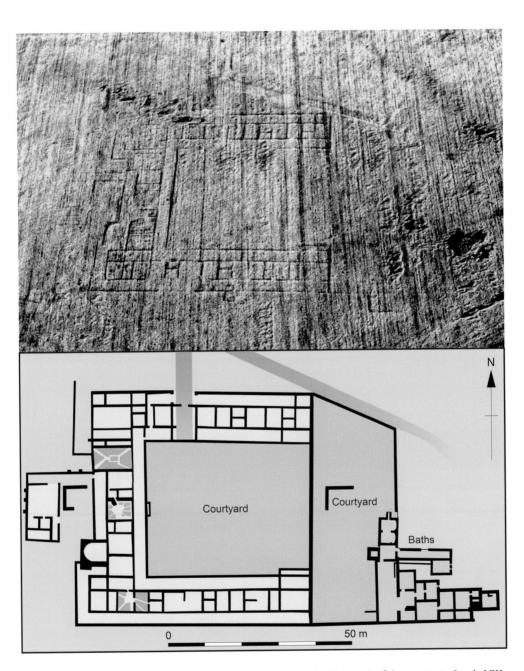

FIGURE 4.9 Aerial photo (top) (courtesy Chris Stanley) and plan (bottom) of the mansio in Insula VIII

# Temples

Although we do not know whether they were paid for from public or private funds, the town probably boasted several temples by the late 1st century. None is of Classical design, built on a raised podium with a colonnaded portico, like the temple of Sulis Minerva in Bath, but all are of Romano-Celtic type, comprising an inner shrine surrounded by a portico or enclosed ambulatory, sometimes simply described as a 'double square' temple. The dedications of statuary by the guild of peregrini found in the small temple in Insula XXXV have already been mentioned (above, p. 80), and it has been persuasively argued that these acts were to commemorate the victory of the Roman army at the battle of Mons Graupius in Scotland in AD 84. This, in conjunction with its 'Iron Age' orientation, points to, but does not prove, a later 1st century date for its construction.

We are on slightly firmer ground regarding the date of the temples in the sacred enclosure which the Antiquaries labelled as Insula XXX at the eastern edge of the town. Two Romano-Celtic temples were early discoveries

FIGURE 4.10 Drone view of late 1st century AD Romano-Celtic temple (temple walls highlighted) in Insula XXX under excavation in 2017

by the Society of Antiquaries there, partly located within the churchyard of St Mary the Virgin, partly within the grounds of the adjacent farmhouse, now the Old Manor House. With a footprint of 22.5 m², the northern of the two is the largest of its kind known from Roman Britain. When were they built? Survey by ground-penetrating radar of the churchyard and grounds of the Old Manor House not only succeeded in finding the eastern side of the temple enclosure wall, but also clear traces of a third temple. Excavation in 2017 confirmed the 1 m wide flint foundations of a 'double square' plan temple and that it was built in the 80s or 90s of the 1st century AD (Fig. 4.10). The standing remains of similar temples in France suggest a height of the inner shrine in excess of 20 m. Whether or not all three were built at the same time, as a group they would have presented an impressive sight, comparable in height to the forum basilica, the middle temple perhaps standing higher than its neighbours. To travellers entering the town from the east towards the end of their journey from London, they would have been silhouetted against the setting sun in the west; to the townspeople the temples would have made a highly visible landmark at the start of the day, a stunning sight as the sun rose behind them in the east.

One more temple may also have originated in the late 1st century. Set in a large walled enclosure in Insula VII, in quite a central position in the town, this temple had a circular shrine, 10.8 m in diameter, set within a 16-sided ambulatory, the whole building being almost 20 m wide (Fig. 4.11). With its deep foundations it is likely that the central shrine rose to much the same height as the temples in Insula XXX, creating another landmark in the town. How the apparently empty enclosed area was used is unknown, but it could well have been a place for the townspeople to meet to take part in the celebration of religious festivals.

Evidence has not survived to associate a particular deity or deities with any of the temples, but a head of the Egyptian god, Serapis, was found re-used as the weight of a press in Silchester village early in the 20th century (Fig. 4.12). Another, unknown deity, in the form of a bronze figurine of a flute player was found in a house in Insula XXIII (Fig. 4.13).

FIGURE 4.11 Plan of temple and temenos in Insula VII

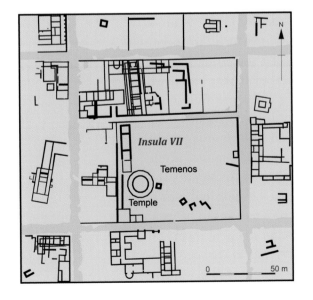

0          5 cm

# Private properties

Turning from public to private, we have a better idea of the development
of domestic dwellings in the late 1st century from the recent excavation of
Insula IX. This revealed that the town house (House 1) which the Society
of Antiquaries had uncovered in 1893 was the last of a succession of three
builds on the same footprint, the first of which was of timber and dated
from the late 1st century (Fig. 4.14). From what we also know from other
neighbouring towns like London and Verulamium, it appears that timber
continued to be the preferred material for building domestic housing in the
late 1st and early 2nd centuries. How many of the domestic houses, whose
masonry foundations were first uncovered by the Society of Antiquaries and
recorded on the 'Great Plan' of the town, were built on the same footprint as
timber predecessors in the late 1st or early 2nd century remains to be seen.
But it is reasonable to assume that this was the case for many of them and
that the plan of the town at the turn of the century was as crowded with
domestic buildings displaying a variety of sizes and plans just as it was two
centuries later.

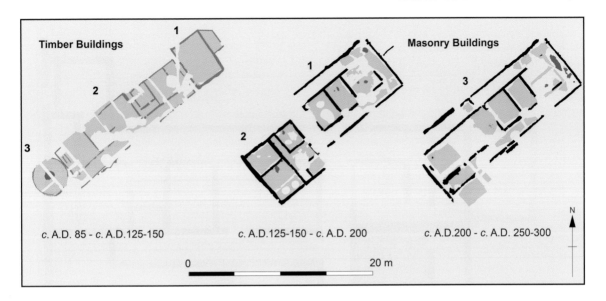

Timber Buildings

Masonry Buildings

1

1

3

2

2

3

N

c. A.D. 85 - c. A.D.125-150       c. A.D.125-150 - c. A.D. 200       c. A.D.200 - c. A.D. 250-300

0                                                                 20 m

FIGURE 4.14 Insula
IX: plans of successive
houses on the site of
House 1 between the
late 1st and the mid-/
late 3rd century

The antiquarian records certainly occasionally report finds which suggest
that they had come across a timber building. A fine example of this is a masonry
house in Insula XIX where remains of a mosaic floor and red tessellated floors
were found beneath its courtyard and aligned with the street grid (Fig. 4.15).
The excavators concluded that they had found a timber-built predecessor
identified as such only by its durable floorings. Excavating such a building
today one would expect to recognise the remains of its wall foundations,
probably in the form of narrow trenches to take sleeper beams, as well as of
any rooms with other forms of flooring, such as of clay or gravel. Although
the excavators did not recover any evidence of date, this house is likely to
have been built before about the 2nd quarter of the 2nd century when, as in
Insula IX, but also in neighbouring towns like Verulamium, domestic houses
began to be built or re-built with masonry foundations.

The house in Insula XIX is important, too, because of the quality of the
mosaic associated with it, which probably decorated the dining suite.
The design of the best-preserved part of the floor includes a great spray
of the wild climbing vine, Mediterranean greenbrier (smilax) shown in
black against a white background (Fig. 4.16). Otherwise, the floor is badly
damaged but the florets enclosed by looped ribbons of a border around the
adjoining, polychrome square employ red and yellow stone tesserae. Like
the marble of the inscriptions, all the types of stone used for the tesserae,
including the hard, white chalk, originated from the Jurassic coast of the
Isle of Purbeck in south-east Dorset.

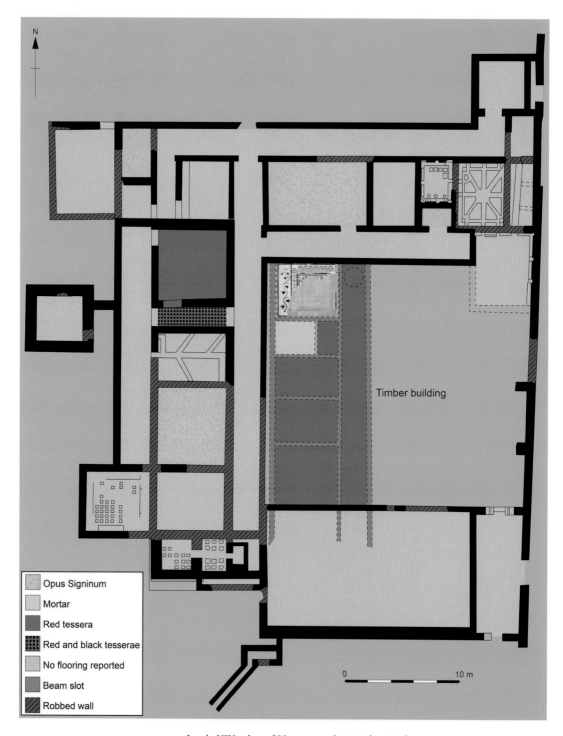

N

Opus Signinum
Mortar
Red tessera
Red and black tesserae
No flooring reported
Beam slot
Robbed wall

Timber building

0                    10 m

FIGURE 4.15  Insula XIX: plan of House 2 and its timber predecessor

## Back to Insula IX

We need to return to Insula IX and the discoveries of the recent excavations
to get a clearer insight into domestic building and domestic life in the late
1st and early 2nd centuries. We have already remarked on the conservative,
'Iron Age' orientation of all the new buildings (Figs 4.17, 4.19). To the north
was a group of three timber-framed buildings, the central one of which was
a multi-roomed, rectangular dwelling, which may have originated as two
separate, three-roomed buildings. The rooms were linked by a corridor or
verandah which ran along their south-east facing side. This is an important
aspect of their plan because it allowed servants or slaves to move around the
building, at the same time giving privacy to the occupants of individual rooms.

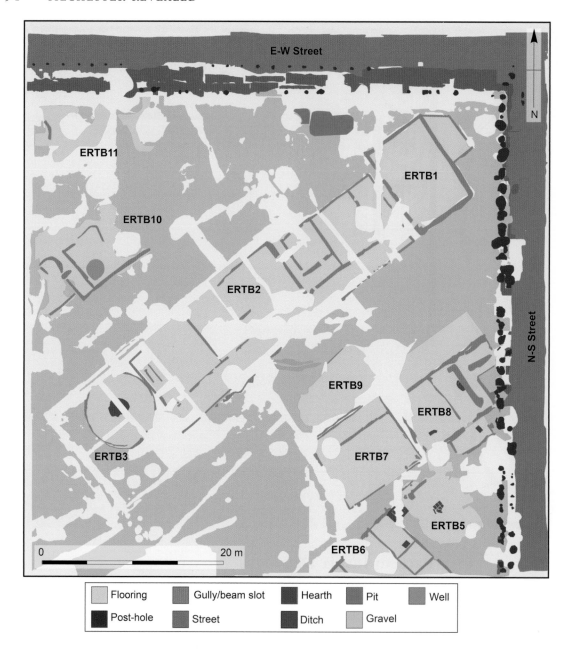

FIGURE 4.17 Insula IX: plan of all late 1st/early 2nd century timber buildings in the excavated area

Apart from its size compared with others in the block, this building would have been distinguished by its red-tiled roof, its neighbours being roofed with thatch. Almost nothing survived of the interior decoration, save a few fragments of painted wall plaster and all that remained of the floors were spreads of gravel or clay. There was no internal hearth but, flanking the house to the north-east, was a single-roomed rectangular building with a large tiled

FIGURE 4.18 Insula IX: the kitchen (ERTB 1 in Fig. 4.17) of the late 1st/ early 2nd century town house under excavation

FIGURE 4.19 Reconstruction of Insula IX in the late 1st and early 2nd century. To the rear, the town house is shown with detached kitchen (right) and roundhouse or possible shrine (left), while, in the foreground is the group of thatched-roofed cottages (by Margaret Mathews)

hearth, centrally located (Fig. 4.18). This building served as the kitchen. A small pit against one wall contained the partial skeleton of a sheep, a possible foundation deposit. A small annexe was later added on the north-east facing wall, its footprint adjusted to respect the ditch draining the east–west street. Whereas the larger room was floored with spreads of gravel and clay, the annexe was furnished with a floor of opus signinum, a pink-red mortar made by adding crushed red tile. This, better appointed space may have served as sleeping quarters for some of the servants. Later, a tiled structure, either a hearth or a setting for a brazier, was built into a corner of the room. A large cess pit full of food waste on the north side of the building provided the clue to its function as a kitchen.

The contents of this pit give us a detailed picture of what the occupants of this household were eating and the variety of food types is impressive. The staples were essentially the same as in the diet revealed by our cess pits half a century earlier, spelt wheat and hulled barley, the cereals processed into flour rather than eaten as whole grains, and peas. Lentils and flax were preserved by mineralisation, in other words they had passed through the human gut. The main sources of meat remained much the same with beef the most important contributor, followed by pork, including from piglets, and mutton and lamb. Interestingly, all body parts of these animals are represented indicating that they were probably slaughtered nearby, rather than procured as joints prepared by specialist butchers. As well as the remains of a considerable number of wild birds, including godwit and passerines, such as sparrow and thrush, there were also hundreds of fish bones, for the most part of freshwater species, particularly of eel, but also salmon, trout and flatfish.

Flavourings are typical of Roman-style cuisine and here dill, but also coriander, celery and mint are prominent among the mineralised seed and plant remains. The same is true of the cultivated fruits especially plum and/or bullace, mulberry, fig and grape, and of wild fruits, especially blackberry, and sloe is also present. It is very likely that mulberry and fig, probably also grape in the form of raisins, were imported, the remaining species locally grown in garden plots or orchards in or around the town. A further insight into the types of food consumed by this household is provided by pollen analysis. The

FIGURE 4.20 Some of the fruits and seeds consumed by the inhabitants of Insula IX in the late 1st/early 2nd century (painting by Jenny Halstead)

pollen of Brassicaceae was present in considerable quantities, suggesting that shoots either close to flowering or actually in flower were eaten. These could have been of native wild species like watercress or charlock (wild mustard), or from a cultivated vegetable similar to broccoli.

The identification of the eggs of whipworm under the microscope recalls the finds from the very earliest deposits next to the bath house and reminds us that not just members of this household in Insula IX, but much of the population of the wider town, were probably infected with whipworm and other intestinal parasites.

Away from the cess pit, at the opposite end of the town house was a third building, a roundhouse, that also had a central hearth and, like the orientation of this trio of buildings, was a reminder of the pre-conquest origins of the town (Fig. 4.21). While two of the three buildings in the group can be readily interpreted as a town house with detached kitchen on one side, the role of the roundhouse remains a puzzle. Was it also residential, or did it, as some of its contents indicate, have some ritual function, perhaps as a domestic shrine? Around the edge of the building were found the following: the interment of a neonate lying on its side in a foetal position, a pit containing the fragmentary remains of a complete cooking pot of Silchester ware associated with the cremated remains of a sheep or goat, and a further shallow pit containing a substantial portion, again fragmentary, of another Silchester ware jar (Fig. 4.22). Three other pits contained charcoal and the cremated and fragmented bone of sheep or goat, while two pits contained only charcoal. The animals

FIGURE 4.21 Insula IX: floor of late 1st/early 2nd century timber roundhouse (ERTB 3 in Fig. 4.17), a possible domestic shrine

are likely to have been sacrifices, their skeletal remains after feasting deliberately cremated at temperatures over 600° centigrade. Although unusual objects are found in the foundations of other buildings, the deposits associated with this roundhouse stand out both in their character and number and point to a religious interpretation for the building. Is there a connection with the distinctive orientation of the buildings, pointing to the mid-summer sunrise/mid-winter solstice? Might they have been the residence of a priest, perhaps a survivor of the druids so persecuted by Rome?

FIGURE 4.22
The neonate, Silchester Ware jar and cremated sheep bone associated with the roundhouse and possible shrine in Insula IX (see Fig. 4.21)

Across the lane or yard to the south and sharing the north-east to south-west alignment were a pair of single-roomed, timber-framed dwellings, both equipped centrally with tiled hearths (Figs 4.19, 4.23). While the geochemistry of the hearth and associated soil of the street-side building reveals a high copper content, the deposits between it and the street were rich in pottery and animal bone, consistent with the waste which might be expected of a food outlet. An initial thought was that the high copper content probably reflected metalworking, but it could also be the result of the intensive use of a copper alloy cooking vessel. The deposits associated with the adjacent building were, by contrast, clean, showing no contamination by metals and other elements. Given its proximity, we could interpret this as the residence of those working in the next door premises, representing a clear separation of commercial and domestic functions and a development on life in the previous century when living and working all took place in the one building in this location. Further privacy for the occupants would have been gained by a corridor which ran around two sides of the building. This space could have been used for storage but it would also have allowed for the separation of servants or slaves from the owners or tenants of the two premises.

Both these buildings have finds incorporated within the make-ups for their floors which suggest deliberate deposition (Fig. 4.24). From one building came the mandible of a young adult female, presumably already in skeletal form, from the other a polished Neolithic flint axe, and both buildings included a complete pig's scapula beneath their floors. Given what they are, it is highly unlikely that these objects could have been deposited by chance, but what might they mean? Perhaps we should think of them as offerings to appease or ward off spirits, while at the same time ensuring a long life for the buildings and their inhabitants.

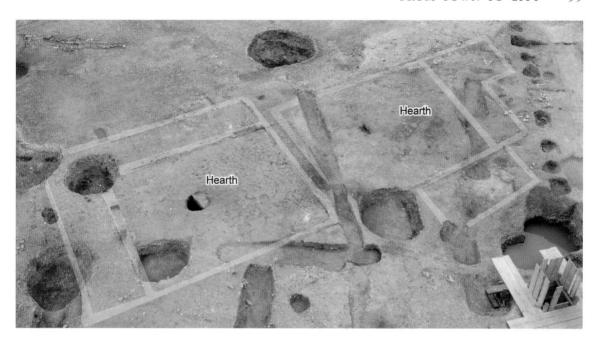

FIGURE 4.23 Insula IX: view over two timber-framed dwellings (ERTBs 7 & 8 in Fig. 4.17) towards the southern limit of the excavated area of Insula IX

FIGURE 4.24 Insula IX: deliberate foundation deposits: lower: mandible of a young adult female; upper: Neolithic polished flint axe

Separated by a narrow alley way on the south side were two other buildings, also on the same north-east to south-west alignment, but belonging to a different property, of which our excavation only caught a part. One, poorly preserved, was another simple, rectangular timber-framed dwelling or workshop with a central hearth, which probably originally fronted on to the street; the other was part of an altogether higher status building, also timber-framed, which extended beyond the limits of the excavated area. One of its rooms was well preserved with its smoothly surfaced floor made of the distinctive material known as opus signinum (Fig. 4.25). Attached to it on one corner was a brick-built furnace, an unusual position if it was designed to heat the room, but remains of burnt animal bone among the ashes suggest it mainly served as an oven. This implies the room was for dining. Later it was divided and a hearth set against the partition.

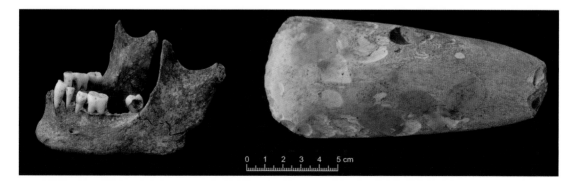

0  1  2  3  4  5 cm

A consistent problem encount-
ered by builders in the town from
now on was the need to consolidate
the ground, which was punctured
by the pits and wells of the Iron
Age and earlier, Roman-period
occupation. Calleva is unusual
in this respect; the great majority
of Roman towns elsewhere in
Britain either had no late Iron Age
precursor or, like Colchester, were
built on fresh ground adjacent to
the existing settlement. In the case
of Calleva, it seems that continuing
to develop the well-drained gravel
promontory occupied by the Iron
Age settlement was more attractive
than starting afresh on a new site.

FIGURE 4.25 Insula
IX: view of room of
timber-framed house
with floor of opus
signinum (ERTB 6 in
Fig. 4.17)

The problem of consolidation was particularly acute in Insula III, immediately
to the west of the forum. Here, re-excavation of the south-east corner of
the block in 2013–14 revealed the unfinished foundations of a late 1st/early
2nd century, timber-framed town house, including the brick footings for a
portico to front onto the main north–south street of the town (Fig. 4.26).
The reason for abandoning the project, the foundations unfinished, can be
seen in their deep slumping into the underlying pits and wells. Despite the
dumping of large quantities of clay, the ground continued to subside into
these features, apparently making the building unviable. It seems that the
problem of the dense underlying occupation led to a decision not to try
and build big properties anywhere else in this block, which appears to have
remained largely undeveloped in the 2nd century. The same problem may
also have affected its immediate and modestly developed neighbour to the
north, Insula II. The only residential dwellings identified in Insula III, a small
cottage on the south side and a simple, rectangular structure on the north
side, have been dated to the late 3rd or 4th century.

A distinctive feature of the town plan is represented by the narrow-
fronted, commercial properties which are particularly conspicuous along
the main east–west street. Carrying all the traffic between London and the
west, this street offered plenty of opportunities for food and other retail
outlets, the competition for space resulting in properties having a narrow

FIGURE 4.26 Insula III: aerial view: the unfinished foundations of a late 1st/early 2nd century building in the south-east corner of the insula are highlighted. The brick footings for the portico can be seen on the right next to the north–south street

street frontage. Certainly, the importance of hearths and ovens to the commerce along this busy highway is emphasised by the high magnetism of these fired clay features which are readily identified by geophysical survey. The hustle and bustle of this particular street is further emphasised by the lack of a comparable density along the main north–south street, or any other in the town. We only have a couple of further insights into the character and function of any of these properties from modern excavation, both fronting on to the north–south street. In Insula IX the one building within the excavated area which gave on to this street probably continued

FIGURE 4.27 Insula
III: 2nd century brick-
built oven

to be used as a food outlet like its 1st century predecessor. However, as we
have seen, analysis of the soil around its central hearth showed a very high
concentration of copper which would suggest it could also have been used
for metalworking. Further south and across the main east–west street in
Insula III, recent re-excavation in 2015 in its north-east corner revealed a
key-hole shaped, brick-built oven, indicating the probable site of a late 1st/
early 2nd century bakery (Fig. 4.27). Close by was a large dump of waste
pointing to the next door property having been used as a blacksmith's shop.

With the new street grid, a new forum basilica, a new bath house, a
(probably) new mansio, at least one new temple, but probably as many as
five, and new private housing and commercial buildings colonising the new
blocks, the late 1st century saw major new development across the town.
Yet more change was to come in the first half of the 2nd century with
widespread re-building in both public and private sectors.

Further sense of new practice in the way the town was run comes from
the evidence for waste disposal. Whereas rubbish pits had been a distinctive
and abundant aspect of the earlier 1st century occupation in Insula IX, from
the end of the century and for at least the following 150 or more years, pitting
became a rarity. Only one large cess pit is associated with the late 1st/early
2nd century town house in Insula IX. We assume it was emptied regularly,
the fills eventually excavated at the beginning of the 21st century representing
the waste from the final weeks of occupation of the house before re-building.
Gone, too, are great dumps within the town, such as those of oyster and
animal bone described in the previous chapter. Now, rubbish seems to have
been disposed of outside the town, onto fields and elsewhere, dumps still
awaiting discovery, leaving the town correspondingly smelling a little sweeter.

CHAPTER FIVE

# The 2nd century:
# Calleva at its peak

...................................................................................................

The most conspicuous build of the early–mid-2nd century was the construction of the masonry forum basilica. Built over the demolished remains of its timber predecessor and occupying a footprint of some 8000 m² (0.8 ha/2 acres), it dominated the central insula of the town and, indeed, the whole town (Fig. 5.1). The basilica – the great hall – was the grandest element of the complex and the ridge of its roof would have stood about 22 m above ground level, almost twice the height of the estimated 12–13 m height of the ranges around the forum (Fig. 5.2). Even they would have been about twice the height of the great majority of the domestic houses and other buildings in the town. The only structures which might have approached, possibly exceeded the height of the basilica, were the temples in Insula VII to the south and Insula XXX at the eastern edge of the town. This was a massive investment in the town and, though archaeological dating can seldom be precise down to a single year, with a coin dated to about AD 122 from the foundations it is tempting to see an association between the Emperor Hadrian's visit to Britain in that same year and the decision to build. Construction would, of course, have taken several years, and the Emperor would never have seen it finished.

Not surprisingly, the masonry forum basilica was built on huge foundations, which survey by ground-penetrating radar shows averaged about 1.5 m deep. Unlike the public baths where the stone was of Wealden Greensand, the forum basilica was built of flint nodules, the nearest available stone, interleaved with courses of brick. Flint is quarried from the chalk, the nearest outcrop of which was only about 7 miles/11 km distant to the south towards

modern Basingstoke. Flint is a very difficult stone to work and, because of its nodular character, completely unsuitable for detailed architectural features. Thus, the great columns and Corinthian capitals of the basilica and the smaller columns of the external and internal porticos around the forum, were mostly carved from the fine and easy-to-work, Oolitic Limestone from the quarries at Bath.

The plan of the building is essentially simple: the forum court was lined on three sides by a portico from which opened rooms, some apsidal in plan. The basilica with its suite of large rooms, including a central, apsidal chamber, closed the fourth side of the forum on its west side, and an external

FIGURE 5.1 Plan and aerial view from the north-west of the early 2nd century masonry forum basilica
(PHOTO COURTESY CHRIS STANLEY)

FIGURE 5.2 Left: view from the north of the basilica under excavation in 1980; right: apse at the south end of the basilica in 1986

FIGURE 5.3
Reconstruction of the
forum basilica, viewed
from the north-east
(BY PETER URMSTON © HISTORIC
ENGLAND ARCHIVE)

colonnade ran around the entire building (Fig. 5.3). This plan resembles
that of the headquarters of a legionary fortress and, like its late 1st century
predecessor, was almost certainly designed by a military architect. This design
is replicated widely elsewhere in Britain and we have solid evidence of very
similar plans from completely excavated examples at Caerwent, the civitas
capital of the Silures in south-east Wales, Caistor-by-Norwich, the civitas
capital of the Iceni in Norfolk, and at Wroxeter, the civitas capital of the
Cornovii in Shropshire. The only exception we can be reasonably confident
of is that at Verulamium, St Albans, which seems to be modelled on designs
to be found in Gaul. One feature of the military building and one that
distinguishes its plan from that of forums on the continent and elsewhere in
the Roman Empire is the lack of a separate temple, a capitolium, dedicated
to the worship of Jupiter, Juno and Minerva.

  In trying to gain further insight into how this great building was used,
we are frustrated by the lack of reliable evidence. It was first excavated by
the Reverend Joyce who, in recording some of the finds in some detail,
speculated about the different functions of the various spaces, for example
those around the forum, identifying some as shops, some as offices. We

should now be cautious about accepting any of these interpretations, not least because they were found on the latest surviving surfaces and may well relate to activity in the building late in or after the end of the Roman occupation. Unlike today, Joyce did not systematically review all the finds, but focused on particular pieces, such as a silver bar which, for him, identified the room in question as that of a jeweller, or groups of pieces, like the collection of coins which suggested to him that one of the rooms was occupied by a banker. Given Joyce's and then the Society of Antiquaries' investigation of the building, it is not surprising that the 1980s excavation of the basilica found few undisturbed deposits. Fortunately, some survived at the northern end, but they relate to the late 3rd and 4th century use of the building. Nothing survived which gave a clue as to the use of the basilica in the 2nd and earlier 3rd centuries; indeed, the lack of any sign of an original, laid floor surface might even suggest that the building was never completed! While the military association with the late 1st century forum basilica is clear both in the construction of the building and in its associated finds, its potential continuation in the life of its successor building is really evident in its complex construction and its ground plan. From the 1980s excavation there are a very few finds associated with its use in the 2nd and 3rd centuries to suggest any continued involvement of military personnel in the administration of the town and civitas. However, there are also other finds of 2nd and 3rd century military metalwork from elsewhere in the town which hint at a continuing military presence (Fig. 5.4).

We might also attribute a re-furbishment of the amphitheatre in the early–mid-2nd century to the visit of Hadrian to Britain in AD 122. The original timbers retaining the seating bank around the arena, now about 50–70 years old and in a considerable state of decay, would have been in need of replacement. This and the possibility of a partial collapse would have influenced

FIGURE 5.4
Third century Roman military roundel from a belt. The letters read OPTIME[MAX]] IMECON – 'Best (and) Greatest, preserve'

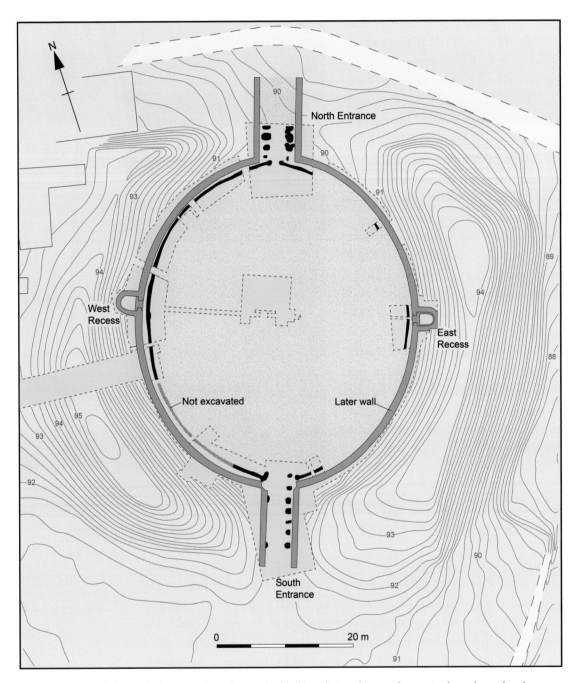

FIGURE 5.5 Plan of the amphitheatre with oval arena (in black) replacing the round arena in the early–mid-2nd century

the decision to re-build. The main change in the early 2nd century was the reconstruction of the arena to make it oval rather than circular in plan so that Calleva would conform with the elliptical or oval plan which had become the norm across the Empire (Figs 5.5–5.6). The new timbers used were of varying sizes, generally less than 0.2 m² in both circular and square cross-section. Considering the amount of construction going on across the town, and given the preference for oak, it is perhaps not surprising that there would have been a shortage of suitable, consistently sized timber and that only material of smaller and variable dimensions was available. Although the overall quantity required would not have been much less than it was for the original build, judging by the variation in size, it is likely that at least some secondhand wood would have been used.

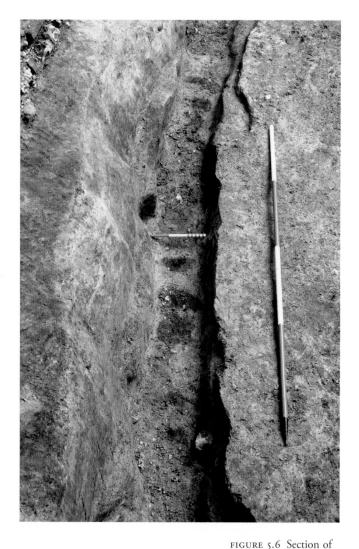

FIGURE 5.6 Section of the arena wall of the amphitheatre showing the dark soil left by the posts of varying size and shape used in the 2nd century re-build

## Water and waste

Although we do not know whether all the inhabitants of Calleva, including slaves, were able to benefit from the entertainments provided at the amphitheatre, or enjoy the baths in Insula XXXIII, these were the only public facilities that we know of that were available to the townspeople. The Antiquaries claimed to have found evidence of a wooden water-pipe which they traced from the ditch outside the town wall to the west. It apparently ran beneath it at a depth of 1.5–2.1 m and for a further 215 m to supply water to Insula III, but it is difficult to see how it would have worked in practice. There was no aqueduct to provide a public source of water and even the baths appear to have relied on nearby springs within the town, the water apparently stored in tanks then lifted by bucket chain, as has been found in London, to provide a regular supply. Otherwise, domestic and commercial needs were provided by wells excavated in individual properties across the town. Water was plentifully available immediately beneath the gravel cap and could be reached at a depth of around 3 m. The Antiquaries found that wells were generally excavated deeper into the underlying clay, to an average depth of about 6 m to provide a decent reservoir of water. Although we have seen an example in Chapter 3 of a 1st century well lined with an old wine barrel, typically linings were made up of oak boards attached to each other by mortise-and-tenon joints strengthened by diagonal struts at the corners and resting on a base plate of oak beams. The internal dimensions of one such well, of early 3rd century date, in Insula IX was 0.65 by 0.7 m (Fig. 5.7). The deepest well so far discovered was of 9 m and in the yard of one of the grandest houses of the town in Insula XIV. Coincidentally, while the great majority of households relied on buckets to lift the water from their well, the other grand house in Insula XIV produced the discarded remains of a force pump, one of only two to have so far been found in Britain. Such a device would have been suitable for a deep well and could in theory have delivered water at the rate of about 40 litres per minute.

Since there was no supply of water to sluice it away, sewage and other waste was disposed of in latrine pits adjacent to dwellings. These were probably emptied regularly, the contents taken out and dumped on fields outside the town. There were exceptions to this behaviour as in the heyday of House 1 in Insula IX between the mid-2nd and the mid-3rd century where no trace of such a latrine pit was found, which suggests that waste

FIGURE 5.7 Base of early 3rd century well in Insula IX lined with oak planks and surrounded by modern shoring

was removed from the house on a daily basis. Besides giving insight into the food consumed by the household, examination of samples prepared for pollen analysis from a latrine pit in Insula IX showed evidence of intestinal infestation by parasites such as whipworm. The latter has already been identified in the earlier occupants of Insula IX, and in the earliest post-conquest deposits in the deep ditch next to the public baths, the implication being that such intestinal infestation was commonplace in Calleva. Rainwater was quickly absorbed by the free-draining gravels upon which the town was built, though the streets were flanked by side ditches and sometimes provided with a central gutter. The baths drained into the stream which rose inside the town and flowed out to the south-east, later through a culvert built into the town wall especially for it.

## Homes and gardens

Of course, the great majority of new build in the early–mid-2nd century were domestic housing and commercial premises, but our problem in trying to understand what these looked like across the town by the middle of the 2nd century is the lack of any dating evidence for them at any phase in their development. We also do not know how many timber buildings may have existed alongside those with masonry foundations which the early excavators were able to recognise. How many houses and other structures were there by the middle of the 2nd century and how did their plans and character differ from their predecessors of the later 1st century and their successors of the 3rd and 4th centuries?

At the moment, almost all we have to go on is the evidence from Insula IX, where the timber-framed town house was replaced by a pair of buildings with masonry foundations (Fig. 5.8). This reminds us of its predecessor which originated as two three-roomed buildings, side by side, but which were later amalgamated to create one house. With the re-build the design reverted to two separate buildings, one of three rooms with a surrounding passage on three sides, the other, square, with lobby and passage giving access individually to its four rooms. There were also traces of a verandah along its south-east elevation This house overlay the roundhouse with all its votive deposits and the make-ups for its floors also contained votives, a bead rim jar from the Alice Holt potteries and a small jar of Silchester ware, each in a separate location (Fig. 5.9). A complete set of toilet instruments incorporated in the make-up of another floor may also have been deposited as a votive. The articulated foot bones of a deer were similarly incorporated beneath a floor of the adjacent house.

The mortared foundations of both houses were of nodular flint, while clay and gravel were used to make up the floors. In a room that overlay an earlier well, packed flint had been used to consolidate the soft fill and prevent subsidence. Final floor surfaces had for the most part long been worn away down to the clay, gravel and flint foundation material, but in the corner of the central room of the northern house were the remains

FIGURE 5.8 Insula IX: aerial view, looking north-east, of the foundations of the two houses representing the first masonry phase of 'House 1' about the mid-2nd century

FIGURE 5.9 Alice Holt jar incorporated as a foundation deposit in the mid-2nd century masonry House 2 in Insula IX

of a tessellated floor made up of small cubes (tesserae) of red brick. It is likely, but we cannot be sure, that this fragment was part of a border which surrounded a patterned mosaic, long since worn away (Fig. 5.10).

This pattern of building, where masonry foundations replaced the use of timber sleeper-beams or posts, can be seen happening in other towns in the south-east, for example, Colchester, London and Verulamium, and so it is very likely that the development which has been observed in Insula IX was widely replicated across Calleva (Fig. 5.11). Very many of the buildings discovered and planned by the Society of Antiquaries will have had their origins in timber in the later 1st century AD, then were re-built with mortared foundations in the early–mid-2nd century. At the same time, as we see in Insula IX, most, if not all, the houses and shops across the town were potentially subject to further change, though some may have been

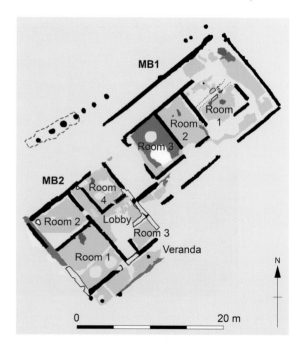

FIGURE 5.10 Plan of the two masonry-founded houses ('House 1') in Insula IX around the mid-2nd century

FIGURE 5.11
Reconstruction of
Insula IX in the mid-
2nd century, view from
the south-east (by
Margaret Mathews)

completely abandoned. With some houses it is possible to speculate how they might have changed over time with the addition of rooms or complete wings. In the case of Insula IX, our two houses were amalgamated around AD 200 to create a large town house, 36 m by 11 m, giving it a footprint of almost 400 m². While there is no sign that either this house or its immediate predecessors had heated rooms, some houses in Calleva probably did have at least one room with underfloor heating (hypocaust) before the end of the 2nd century. The floor would have been supported on closely spaced stacks of tiles, which allowed warm air to circulate. This was then taken up the walls and out beneath the eaves into the atmosphere through pipes constructed of flue tiles rectangular in cross-section.

Insula XIV contains two of the largest and finest houses in Calleva, both showing signs of complex histories of development. The final plan of House 1 consists of four ranges around a central courtyard, but it looks as if the eastern range was built first, the other three added later (Fig. 5.12). The eastern range was lavishly decorated with a suite of mosaics that on stylistic grounds appear to be second century in date (Fig. 5.13). They show considerable signs of wear and repair and probably remained in use into the 5th century and until the final abandonment of the house. It was certainly not the only house in Silchester to have been furnished with mosaic floors

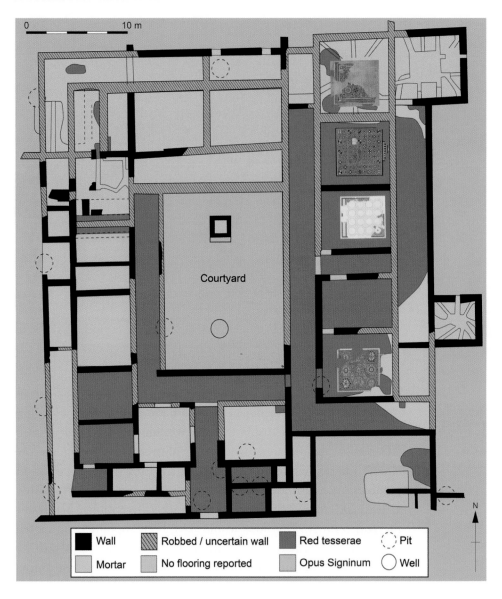

FIGURE 5.12 Plan of
House 1 in Insula XIV

in the 2nd century (see Fig. 1.8) but, as we have seen in Insula IX, much
has been lost to wear and tear. Re-excavation of a town house, such as those
in Insula XIV, would achieve a great deal, not least the unravelling of the
development of two grand houses and confirmation of the date of their
mosaic floors, but also how the open spaces of inner and outer courtyards
were used. Were there gardens here, perhaps?

The best clue for the existence of gardens, or at least borders, comes
from finds of box leaves. Clement Reid identified three instances from
waterlogged samples from the Antiquaries' excavations, to which we can

FIGURE 5.13 Mosaics
from House 1, Insula
XIV
(COURTESY OF STEPHEN
COSH AND DAVID NEAL, BY
PERMISSION OF THE SOCIETY OF
ANTIQUARIES)

add a fourth from a well deposit of about AD 200 from Insula IX. Along
with herbs and flavourings like coriander, dill and mint, and root and leaf
vegetables such as celery, brassicas and turnips, it is also highly likely that
fruit trees, especially plum and bullace, were grown widely across the town.
Otherwise the plant record from 2nd and 3rd century Insula IX suggests a
neglected look to the open spaces among the various buildings within the
block. Heavily worn areas would have been quite free of vegetation but,
where there was less trampling, weeds like knotgrass, small nettle, chickweed
and fat hen would have grown. In the rarely visited corners tall herbs typical
of waste ground like stinging nettle, broad-leaved dock, blackberry and elder
would have flourished.

There was more to the town than houses of masonry construction –
building in timber did not stop in the 2nd century. At the north end of
the pair of early 2nd century houses in Insula IX the earlier timber-framed
building was retained and extended. While it may have initially continued to
serve as the kitchen for one or both houses, microscopic study of the floors
revealed traces of herbivore dung and other indications that, as the structure
decayed, the space came to be used to accommodate domestic animals like
cattle or sheep. A little way to the south, within the excavated area of Insula
IX and fronting onto the north–south street, traces of another rectangular
timber building were discovered. If we extrapolate from this excavation, it
is likely that many of the apparently blank areas on the town plan were
occupied by timber buildings which the early excavators did not have the
experience to recognise. Not knowing how densely built up the town was

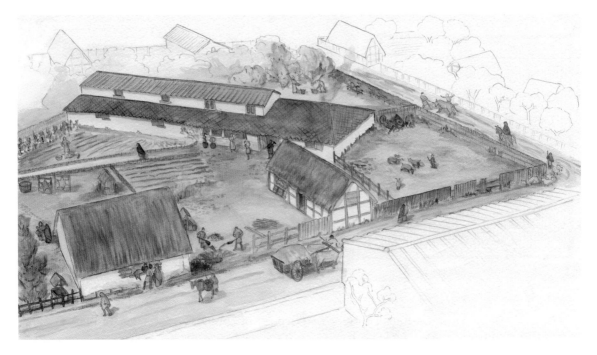

at any one time, or which buildings were occupied by people rather than used in other ways, such as for workshops, storage, or to accommodate animals, makes estimating the population of the town and how that may have changed over time extremely difficult (Fig. 5.14).

FIGURE 5.14
Reconstruction of life in Insula IX in the early 3rd century (by Margaret Mathews)

## Urban economy

The second century was a period of stability in Britain when town life appears to have flourished. If we are correct in supposing that the town houses, commercial premises and other buildings uncovered by the early excavators developed in the way that has been demonstrated in Insula IX and elsewhere in other southern towns, we can begin to profile the town's population. In the private sphere the most distinctive types of buildings are domestic houses, which occur across the town in a wide variety of sizes and plan forms, and the narrow-fronted shops or shops-cum-workshops, which are particularly evident along the main east–west street.

An important question in trying to understand the people, their lives and the economy of a town like Calleva is the extent to which it depended on the wealth derived from country estates, rather than on occupations developed within the town. If town life was considered desirable in itself, then it might attract landowners to invest in a town house, while the income from their estate supported their household day-to-day. These are the people who were expected to run the town including the building, repair and the servicing of infrastructure like the amphitheatre, forum basilica and public baths as well, perhaps, as the inn (mansio) to accommodate travellers on official business using the imperial posting service, the cursus publicus. Such people may well have been the owners of some of the larger houses within the town.

Alternatively, the proceeds, including rents, derived from commercial premises might have been sufficient to support a town-house style of living for some and it seems very likely that smaller properties probably belonged to those whose families and slaves worked in the town. Indeed, the largest source of wealth for the town, other than country estates, is likely to have come from the commerce generated by the through traffic, with travellers needing food and accommodation for themselves, their vehicles and their mounts. As we have seen in Chapter 4, Calleva was at the hub of roads leading in all directions but, judging by the density of premises along the east–west street, it was the traffic between London and the west and, thereby, to a great variety of destinations which was the most important. This is reflected in a document known as the *Antonine Itinerary* which is thought to date to the beginning of the 3rd century, but incorporating earlier information. It lists a series of routes along the roads across the Empire of which 15 concern Britain. Recalling the central role we suggest it played in the aftermath of the Boudican revolt (Chapter 3), Calleva is the starting point of three routes: west to the legionary fortress at Caerleon via Cirencester and Gloucester; to the same destination but via Bath and Sea Mills at the mouth of the River Avon for the crossing of the Severn Estuary; and south-west to Exeter via Winchester and Dorchester. It is also incorporated in one other route from Chichester to London via Winchester and Silchester.

Geophysical survey can help us map the intensity of through traffic by detecting the higher magnetism created by burnt structures, like kilns and hearths. The density of such 'hot spots', particularly noticeable along the east–west street, indicates the importance of businesses like bakeries, breweries and other food outlets. Traffic through the town would also have generated secondary occupations such as carpentry and blacksmithing to repair vehicles, harnesses and such like. Such occupations would, of course, have been in demand by the townspeople themselves. For those travellers, like merchants, not on official business, overnight accommodation would have been required for them and their horses. Some of the buildings set back behind the main streets may well have provided guest rooms and stabling. We can only imagine the kind of impact a unit of infantry or cavalry traveling to or from the legionary fortress at Caerleon might have had on the life of the town, but such troop movements were probably infrequent.

Apart from pottery, to date we cannot identify any crafts or industries whose products at this time were both made in Calleva and used exclusively in the town. This is largely because many objects, such as spoons, follow an Empire-wide style, even if they were made locally. Everyday objects, such as iron tools and the fittings and fixings used in the building and furnishing of houses would certainly have been made by resident blacksmiths, but this is hard to prove as the forms of these functional objects do not vary. However, if roofing tiles and other ceramic building material can be shown to have been manufactured near the town, as they were at Little London, it is likely that a whole variety of day-to-day items including clothing and footwear were also made within the town.

While some occupations like ironmaking, blacksmithing or butchery leave easily recognisable waste behind, others, such as brewing or carpentry, where their waste does not survive well in the archaeological record, are hard to pin down to a particular location. The gathering and supply of wood for fuel must have been a major occupation but only visible through deposits of ash and charcoal. A large deposit of iron forging waste discovered in the north-east corner of Insula III in 2015 is probably the only clue that we have for the location of a blacksmith in the 2nd century, but there must have been several others. While butchered animal bone is a commonplace find across the town, the location of any butchers' premises is hard to pin down. Indeed, it is possible that butchers were at least partly itinerant carrying out their work in individual properties across the town. That there were specialists is indicated by the particular manner with which cattle carcases were butchered and by the discovery of large dumps of the unwanted parts of the skeleton – skulls, jaws and feet – which suggest they derived from a single source. One such mid-1st century deposit was found in the south-west corner of the town.

Animal bones and skins also had further uses. The bones could be used for a wide variety of purposes from handles for knives and other tools to pins, needles, spindle-whorls, dice, hinges, etc. Boneworking waste, consisting of the shoulder blades of sheep from which flat rings had been cut, was recovered from a pit in Insula XVI and a deposit of some 60 horn cores from a pit in Insula XXXVI hints at the proximity of workers in horn. A very large deposit of cattle jaws found in the north-west corner of Insula VI and probably of later 1st century date may be waste material from hides prepared for tanning. This raises the question: with plentiful water in the south-east quarter, was tanning an important industry of the town? It is, though, a foul-smelling industry and would usually have been carried out well away from domestic dwellings.

Like brick making, pottery making is an occupation whose products are often distinctive and easy to recognise as it leaves behind the remains of durable kilns and mounds of wasters. Where these have been found associated with towns they are located outside the heart of the settlement, on the margins or in the suburbs, as for example at Colchester, London and St Albans. These industries produced a range of wares including the distinctive mortarium, a vessel used for preparing food and commonly stamped with the maker's name, examples of which can be found widely across the province. At Silchester pottery making appears to have been on a much smaller scale, probably because, as we shall see (p. 121), of major competition from an industry located only 15 miles (24 km) from the town. The remains of kilns were found a little to the north of the town, which produced plain domestic wares, such as bowls, dishes, jars and flagons, but

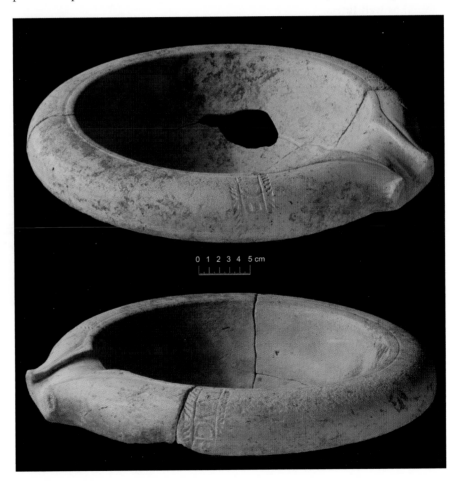

0 1 2 3 4 5 cm

FIGURE 5.15 An early 2nd century mortarium made near Verulamium (St Albans) by the potter Matugenus. The rim is stamped either side of the spout Matuge(nus) Fecit (Matugenus made it)

not mortaria (Fig. 5.15), at the beginning of the 2nd century. To date, these Silchester-made vessels have only been found within the town and, like the pottery production at Little London in the 1st century, this activity seems to have been short lived.

If Calleva, the town, was not a great exporter of pottery, it was certainly a great consumer of it. And, thanks to the way it has been possible to recognise the production centres of a wide range of pottery types, we can see from where, whether from within Britain or from overseas, and in what quantities, the pottery found at Silchester was imported. First, there were the amphorae which brought luxury drink and foodstuffs from the Mediterranean world, particularly olive-oil from southern Spain and wine from southern France, though together representing only a very small proportion (2–3%) of the pottery assemblage as a whole. Other much more perishable containers brought wine into the town, such as the barrels made from silver fir (see Fig. 1.11), but they are only recognised when they survive in wet conditions re-used as well-liners.

By the middle of the 2nd century most of the town's drinking vessels and tableware were still imported. The main types of tableware – cups, bowls, dishes, platters – all with a very distinctive semi-glossy, red finish were imported, chiefly from workshops at Lezoux in the centre of France (Fig. 5.16). Despite its distance from the town, this production centre was second only in importance to the very local Alice Holt pottery. Beakers for drinking,

FIGURE 5.16
Black-slipped beaker made at Lezoux, central France, by the potter Libertus, early 2nd century. Decorated with figures (from left to right) of Venus, Kore and Demeter, a seated woman, Bacchus and two Bacchantes, and Neptune supporting a mask. OF(ficina) LIBERTI, the workshop of Libertus can be read

0    1    2 cm

sometimes decorated with hunting scenes, were also imported from potteries in the Argonne region of northern France and from Cologne on the Rhine. Vessels for the storage, preparation and cooking of food were made much more locally. Indeed, over half of all the pottery consumed in Calleva at this time was made in potteries in Alice Holt Forest, near Farnham, Hampshire, 15 miles (24 km) to the south-east of the town. This industry had begun to develop around or just before the Roman conquest of AD 43, but it had become Silchester's main source of domestic pottery by the end of the 1st century (see Fig. 3.22). It remained a major supplier to Silchester and to south-east England more widely until the end of Roman Britain in the 5th century. The town also regularly received supplies of pottery, particularly flagons and mortaria, from the major production centre situated between London and St Albans and from that located on the outskirts of Oxford; it also bought in cooking wares made at Poole Harbour in south-east Dorset. Between them these regional sources accounted for about 15% of the pottery consumed around the middle of the 2nd century.

This mix of local, regional and imported pottery is probably also mirrored in the origins of other goods, such as glassware, whose place of manufacture is difficult to tie down. While window glass, large bottles and some of the plainer vessels were probably made in Britain, finer cups, bowls and jugs designed for drinking and the table, usually with close and sometimes numerous parallels on the continent, are likely to be imports. A painted glass bowl from the forum basilica is a very rare find indeed. Probably a product of Mediterranean workshops, the best parallels are to be found among the glass vessels from the royal residence at Begram, Afghanistan! Rare also, as far as finds in Britain are concerned, is the imported square-bodied 'Mercury flask' from Insula IX. A continental origin is probably the case for certain bronze vessels, such as the jug with its handle in the form of a human foot, examples of which are found in small numbers across the northern provinces of the Empire, or a razor with a beautiful ivory handle depicting mating dogs (Figs 5.17, 5.19).

How goods which were not made in the town reached their consumers is unclear. We do not know whether there were regular markets in the town or whether specialist shops supplied by travelling merchants were responsible. Buildings identified as pottery shops, for example, have been found in the wreckage left by the Boudican destruction in Colchester, London and St Albans, but glassware and spices were also among their stock. Silchester is notable for the apparently low density of settlements, especially of villas, in its vicinity and this challenges the idea that it served as a market town encouraging the development of settlement in the countryside around it. Part of the explanation for this lies in the character and quality of the soils with clay lands to the south and east and agriculturally poor heathland to the west and north. It is not until the lighter soils on the chalk 6–7 miles (9.6–11.3 km) to the south around Basingstoke and the alluvial soils of the Kennet and Thames valleys, 5–10 miles (8–16 km) to the north, are reached that the density of settlement increases. Nevertheless, the towns people required feeding and it is doubtful whether gardens and orchards within the town or land farmed within easy reach of the town would have been sufficient. That there was plenty of pasture as well as arable close to the town is shown by the presence of cereals, particularly wheat, and non-cereal grasses in the pollen record. While individual estates were probably responsible for the food consumed by their own households and dependants within the town, there would have been others, not least the smaller households and those running outlets selling food and drink to travellers, who would have surely looked to a regular – daily or weekly – market for their supplies.

With its excellent communications the town would also have been the place where estate owners could sell their harvest to meet demands, such as supplying the army in Britain and overseas, over and above those of Calleva itself. Whether the courtyard of the building we call the forum basilica was the market place where such transactions took place or whether other, open spaces within the town were used remains to be established. Important business between merchant and estate owner would also have taken place in private houses. Cereals and livestock, the most important products of the countryside, were bulky and valuable commodities, the grain likely to be stored on property within the town owned by the estate from which it came, the animals to be sold for slaughter would also have been kept in barns inside the town or secure paddocks outside the town. If much high-level business took place on a one-to-one basis within the town, there was also a context for all those across the civitas, the administrative territory governed from Calleva, to come to the town at least once a year to pay their taxes. This would have been delivered to the offices in the

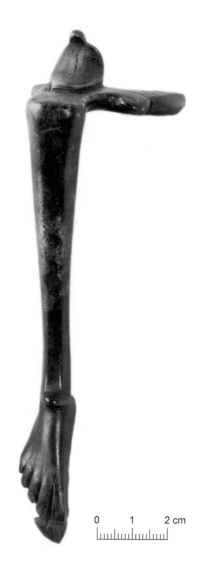

FIGURE 5.17 Handle in the form of a human foot of an imported later 1st or 2nd century bronze jug

forum basilica, which was also the place where judicial matters were resolved. Occasions when taxes had to be paid or when grain had to be sold after harvest may well have coincided with seasonal festivals and markets which attracted people from right across the civitas.

For business purposes record keeping would have been an essential part of everyday life for the great majority of households across the town. Such clues that we have for now about literacy and the nature of town life more generally around the mid- and later 2nd century come from the Insula IX excavation and what we can learn of life in and around the two town houses which merged into one by about AD 200. There are plenty of styli, instruments for writing on wooden writing tablets inset with wax, as well as three seal boxes, a samian inkwell and a wooden writing tablet. We do not know if the skills of reading, writing and numeracy were handed down within the household or whether there were dedicated teachers within the town, but they would have been essential to everyday business and communications (Fig. 5.21).

## Town and country

In reconstructing the life of the inhabitants of the Insula IX town house, we should consider their relationship with the countryside. This might mean no more than access to fields close to the town, but some of the wealthier Callevans would have had an out-of-town estate. The insects from the one well of this period within the excavated area indicate that herbivores – cattle, sheep, horses – were kept in the vicinity. This is supported by finds of the remains of neonatal sheep/goat and pig and the evidence for herbivores stalled in the decaying timber building in the north-east corner of the block. Were these animals reared and kept by the people living on Insula IX for their own consumption, perhaps being driven outside the town to forage each day, or had they been raised on country estates and were penned on Insula IX for only a short time before being sold on for use elsewhere in the town or beyond? On the other hand, when it comes to the question of how grain moved from the countryside to market and whether it was stored in premises around the town, the absence of grain pests indicates that it was not stored in this part of the insula. However, the scarcity of any charred chaff deriving from the processing of grain shows a major change from the previous situation and may well be linked to the rarity of hand mills from this and later periods of occupation. The two phenomena may be linked to the development of animal and water powered mills that could supply flour to households which then no longer had to acquire whole grain from the countryside and grind it themselves. Or, with hand mills no longer available, did people have to pay for the grain they had grown themselves to be processed at a town mill?

Another notable change in the 2nd century in Insula IX is the rarity of equipment related to spinning and the making of textiles. This is particularly evident in the scarcity of spindle-whorls which were such a dominant feature of 1st century AD late Iron Age and Roman finds. We know that cloth production could be state-controlled, but was even the low-technology domestic occupation of spinning now centrally or estate controlled?

Metalworking, on the other hand, appears to have been on the rise from the later 2nd century. Present in Insula IX, but with deposits continuing beyond the excavated area, is ironworking waste in the form of slags derived from smelting ore in small bowl furnaces and hammerscale, the spatters of fine particles created by smithing. These suggest that tools and iron hardware were made and repaired close by. Further, within one of the town houses were found microscopic as well as geochemical traces of the working of gold, silver and, perhaps copper, though the concentrations of the latter were not so great as they were from the late 1st/early 2nd century workshop in Insula IX. We cannot tell whether this is waste from, say, the making of jewellery or from the melting down of precious family objects to sell to keep the household going. Though the working of precious metals appears to have continued after the amalgamation of the two houses into one, it did not persist into the late Roman occupation of the insula.

## Life and death

As well as domestic animals being kept in Insula IX, there was evidence for the beginning of a very noisome activity, the smells from which would have drifted around the neighbourhood. This involved the heavy fragmentation of the limb bones of large mammals for the extraction of oil from the marrow which could be suitable for use in cosmetics, soap or medicinal salves. Further boiling of the bone fragments produced grease and glue from the bone collagen, and the shattered fragments could be used to make small bone objects such as hairpins. Another animal-related occupation in Insula IX evident in the later 2nd and 3rd centuries concerns dogs. There is a concentration of remains in the south-east of the excavated area where

FIGURE 5.18 Dog bone with fine knife marks from Insula IX; evidence of dogs skinned for their pelts

(PHOTO IAN R. CARTWRIGHT)

fine knife marks show that these animals were skinned so that their pelts could be used (Fig. 5.18). Whether this was an occupation specific to one household or more widespread within the town, only extensive further excavation within the town will determine.

One of the most remarkable finds from Insula IX may relate to the end of this activity. In one of the pits into which the dogs' remains had been deposited was found a razor with an ivory handle carved with an image of mating dogs (Fig. 5.19). Beside it was the skeleton of a puppy carefully arranged in a position as if it were sleeping and close by in the pit were the bones of a raven, a bird traditionally associated with death and the afterlife, as well as the remains of other dogs (Fig. 5.20). While these might have been thrown into the pit along with the other domestic rubbish found in it, it is hard to explain the positioning of the dog and its close association with the razor as other than deliberate. Are we seeing evidence of a sacrifice, perhaps instigated by a significant event in the household, such as the death of the peltmaker or his departure from his cottage?

We must wonder how representative are our households in Insula IX. Within close proximity of each other we find the relatively prosperous, the

FIGURE 5.19 Imported
folding knife or razor of
2nd or early 3rd century
date with ivory handle
carved in the form of
two mating dogs
(PHOTO IAN R. CARTWRIGHT)

occupants of our modest town house, living alongside messy and smelly occupations, a situation reminiscent of living conditions in 1st century Pompeii and likely to be repeated across Calleva. At the same time it appears that the inhabitants within the excavated area were reliant on only one, shallow well and of limited capacity. Was this sufficient for the various needs of all the occupants, particularly for those processing the animal bone or working in the smithy, or was there another well just beyond the limits of the excavation? How important was water, rather than, say, ale (or wine)

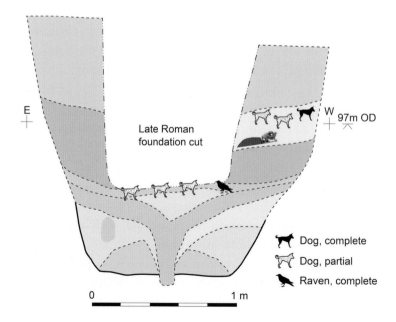

FIGURE 5.20 Profile of
the early 3rd century
pit in Insula IX which
contained the complete
skeleton of a dog, the
ivory-handled razor, a
raven and the remains
of several other dogs

0 1 2 3 4 5 cm

in the daily life of the individual? Another feature of life in Insula IX in the later 2nd and early 3rd centuries is the lack of rubbish pits or even a single, dedicated cess pit of the type found both earlier in the 2nd century and later, in the 4th. Most of our knowledge of the life of the inhabitants at this time therefore comes from the rubbish dumped in the wells when they were abandoned and not from purpose-dug cess or rubbish pits. Such acts of filling probably represent only days or weeks in the life of the insula leaving the question of how domestic rubbish and toilet waste were normally disposed of day-to-day. Was there, as suggested in the previous chapter, an organised disposal of rubbish managed by the town's ordo, or was it down to the discretion of households, those with servants or those who could otherwise afford to have it taken by others and dumped outside the town to fertilise the fields? Indeed, there is not one dedicated cess or rubbish pit associated with the occupants of the Insula IX town house between about the middle of the 2nd and the middle of the 3rd century! However, the occasional instance of the abandonment of a well provided a perfect

FIGURE 5.22
Reconstructed view
across the town from
the east as it might
have appeared in the
later 3rd century after
the construction of the
city wall
(BY IVAN LAPPER © HISTORIC
ENGLAND ARCHIVE)

opportunity for the dumping of domestic rubbish. Care over waste disposal
may have also paid a dividend in terms of the health of the community.
Nevertheless, the 2nd century continued to see evidence of infant burial
in Insula IX, although, when only one or two bones occurred in a single
context, it is possible that they were disturbed from earlier burials.

Where were the limits of the town beyond which the dead could be
buried and the rubbish could have been dumped? The only clue that we
have is the location of what became the town gates in the 3rd century (Fig.
5.22). These might have been built first as monumental arches with a fence
or slight ditch to link one with the other and so mark the limits of the
lived-in space of the town. Certainly, the street grid does not extend beyond
this proposed boundary, though there is ribbon development stretching
out along the major roads, particularly the main east–west routes, and in
other towns the cemeteries tended to lie just beyond the built-up areas and
alongside the main roads. The few burials that we know of which date or
probably date to the 2nd century all lie further out from the settled area. The

predominant rite at this time was cremation and such burials of late 1st/early 2nd century date have been found cut into the rampart in Rampier's Copse and in the field outside the Sandy's Land rampart to the north-west of the town. Patches of calcined bone, possibly human, found in the ploughsoil east of the town hint at the location of another cremation cemetery. Clearly there is much more to learn about the 2nd century cemeteries of Calleva, but the nature of the burial rite – cremation – destroys much of the information that we could learn from skeletal remains.

Burials take us back to thinking about the individual and what we might learn of a person's life in Calleva. First, we have the evidence recovered from within the town and the incidence of infant burials, mostly of neonates, that we have seen in Insula IX to remind us of probable high infant mortality. Then, as an indicator of the general health of the population, we have the recurrent incidence of intestinal parasites like whipworm and maw-worm in cess pits, which points to widespread poor health and which may well have affected mortality rates. In the absence of 2nd century skeletal data we can draw on later Roman skeletal evidence from cemeteries in other towns in southern Britain. This indicates that even for those who survived the first 3 years, life expectancy beyond the mid-40s was assured for only barely a third of the population with fewer still, less than 10% living to or beyond their 60s. About a fifth died as young or prime adults between the end of their teens and their mid-30s. Moving from the individual we can now consider the population of the town as a whole.

Estimating the size of the population is fraught with difficulties. Although we have the plans of many buildings from across the town, we do not know how many were occupied at any one time, nor do we know how many timber buildings stood among those with masonry foundations. As to how many people lived in a house, much depends on how many had an upper storey. Earlier we saw that the amphitheatre, when first built, might have accommodated up to about 7250 individuals, though the 2nd century re-modelling might have reduced the numbers a little. Although an estimate as low as 600–750 has been offered in the past, it is hard to see how the town could have been viable with a population of that size; for now we will reckon with a population in the 2nd century of about 7000.

# CHAPTER SIX

# Calleva defended

Since the abandonment of the late Iron Age defence, the Inner Earthwork, Silchester had developed as an open settlement, but circumstances at the end of the 2nd century brought about radical change with the construction of a new defensive circuit. This work had a profound influence on the subsequent development of the town. Precisely what led to it is open to debate but Silchester was one among many large and small towns which were similarly defended at this time. One explanation is that the defences were a response to what was described as the greatest war in the reign of Emperor Commodus (AD 176–193) when barbarian tribes broke through the northern frontier to threaten the rest of the province. Victory was celebrated in 184, and then again the following year! Another possibility is the assassination of Commodus in 193 and the subsequent struggle for control of the empire. One of the contenders was the governor of Britain, Clodius Albinus, who proclaimed himself Augustus in 196 and took an army out of Britain to Gaul to fight his rival, Septimius Severus. Leaving behind a vulnerable province it would have been a sensible precaution for him to authorise the towns to equip themselves with appropriate defences. Severus eventually defeated Albinus in a battle outside Lyons early in AD 197. Only the discovery of preserved wooden piling beneath one or more of these towns' defences with the potential of producing an exact year of felling through dendrochronological dating would allow us to discriminate between these two possibilities (or any other for that matter), but the nature of Silchester's defences is consistent with a rapid response to an emergency.

Calleva was enclosed by a rampart built from the soil and clay excavated from two concentric ditches which fronted it (Figs 6.1–6.2). The rampart originally stood some 3–4 m high and was probably topped by a timber

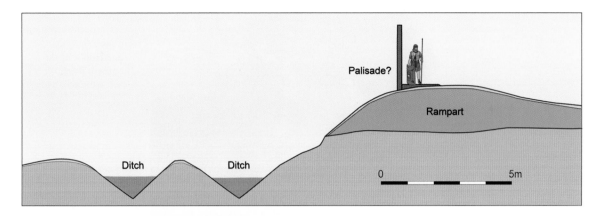

*Top:* FIGURE 6.1 Reconstructed profile of the earthen rampart and associated ditches which defended Calleva around AD 200

*Bottom:* FIGURE 6.2 Excavating through a section of the town rampart of c. AD 200 down to the underlying occupation in 1974

palisade with gates potentially of timber. Altogether the circuit is about a mile and a half (*c.* 2.5 km) in length and the area enclosed about 107 acres (43.2 ha). It was eventually replaced by the town wall (below). At first sight, its construction might be thought as one which could have taken a long time, possibly years, to complete. However, it is much easier to construct a defence like this than it is to build a wall with materials such as brick and mortar which, even if available locally, have to be specially made or prepared or, in the case of stone, carted in from a greater distance. Depending on the size of the labour force the rampart could have easily been built within a year: a gang of 300 could probably have constructed it in less than 6 months.

As suggested in the previous chapter, the four main gates may have been built earlier as part of a scheme to mark the boundary of the settlement to separate it from the areas beyond where the dead could be buried. All were built of masonry and all are earlier than the construction of the town wall: to east and west they were provided with double carriageways flanked by towers, matching the importance and volume of traffic along the east–west route to and from London; the North and South

gates, however, were only single carriageways (Figs 6.3–6.5). One might
have expected a similar gate where the road to Old Sarum and Dorchester
left the town but there are no obvious remains. Instead there may have
been a simple passageway for pedestrians, similar to the one giving access
to the amphitheatre on the north-east side and the gate on the south-east
side, which gave passage to a building just outside the walls, one probably
connected with the mansio. As seems to have been the case with the latter,

FIGURE 6.5 The south-east (later blocked) postern gate under excavation in 1976, looking into the town

the lesser gates could have been initially constructed in timber, consistent with a response to an emergency. However, evidence from the North Gate excavation in 1991 indicated that the roadway was initially blocked by the rampart running across it. The same may have been true of both the gate giving access to the road to the south-west and the gate to the amphitheatre, as there is no trace of structures comparable to either the North or South gates or even of the simple, brick-built gate on the south-east side. It would certainly have made sense to have limited the potential weak points in the defences, especially the minor gates.

This rampart, very reminiscent of Iron Age defences, was a makeshift affair, designed to respond to what, hopefully, would have been a short-lived emergency. We do not know how long it was maintained but, for a defence to be consistent with a town of Calleva's status, something more permanent was required. In the later 3rd century, between about 260 and 280, a major project was begun to address a perceived need for a new defence of the town. This was a turbulent time in the empire with the establishment of the breakaway Gallic Empire of AD 260–274 in the west.

Calleva's town wall is one of the great monuments of Roman Britain. The complete circuit, almost 1.5 miles in length (2.5 km), is preserved and accessible to visitors, with the most impressive stretch around the south side of the town (Figs 6.6–6.8). Its construction involved a huge amount of work both in the procurement of materials and the building itself. A section of the wall by the South Gate survives to a height of some 4.5 m, a little

a

b

FIGURE 6.6 a: The city wall near the South Gate in 1975 before conservation; b: a stretch of the southern wall after conservation looking eastwards

(COURTESY JOHN R. L. ALLEN)

FIGURE 6.7 Impression of hobnailed boot in mortar on the southern wall

more than half of its estimated original height of about 6 m. It is nearly 3 m wide at the base, but this reduces to about 2.3 m at 2.5 m above the base. At intervals of about 60 m the basal thickness is carried to the full height of the wall to create internal, shallow, buttress-like projections, each about 3.7 m long. Though no trace now survives, it would have been topped by a parapet about 1.8 m high. It has been calculated that the volume of material required was about 40,000 m³ and that the building of the wall alone might have taken some 90,000 man-days, perhaps 5–10 years, the length of time dependant on the size of the work force and the seasonality of the work. This estimate does not allow for the procurement of the necessary materials, nor for the excavation of the 14 m wide, 4 m deep, defensive ditch in front

FIGURE 6.8
Reconstructions of a:
the North Gate by Ivan
Lapper; b: the South
Gate by Peter Urmston
(© HISTORIC ENGLAND)

of it. This is particularly well preserved in the woodland around the south-west section of the wall circuit.

Even now, in its much-reduced state, the wall makes an impressive sight, particularly as you approach it coming up Church Lane from the south in winter when the vegetation is down. At the end of the 3rd century, however, it would have completely transformed the look of the town: as travellers drew near little else of the town would have been visible other than the wall and the gates towering above.

The course the wall takes is exactly that of the earthen rampart of around AD 200, the front of which was cut away to make way for the new build. The wall incorporated the existing four main gates and the south-east postern. Only at the south-west, where the road leads to Old Sarum, and by the amphitheatre is there evidence of newly built, but slighter gates. Intriguingly, geophysical survey in St Mary's churchyard points to a further, previously unknown gate and passageway on the eastern side, subsequently completely blocked. The internal, buttress-like projections where the basal thickness of the wall was carried to its full height, may have supported interval towers. Although we cannot be precise about dates, work started, as mentioned above, between 260 and 280. Had the work started a little later, in the 280s, then it might be expected that the wall would have been built with integral external bastions of the kind which feature in the late Roman coastal forts of south-east Britain, such as at Portchester Castle at the head of Portsmouth Harbour, Hampshire, built in the 280s and 290s. Completion then can be estimated to have been between 270 and 290, very probably by the early-to-mid-280s.

## Labour and materials

The wall is largely built of flint, but what makes it particularly distinctive is the use of large stone slabs to provide the string or bonding courses, every 4–6 rows of flint nodules, instead of the more usual brick. While the flint could be obtained locally from the Chalk, outcropping only 6–7 miles (9.7–11.2 km) south of the town, the stone used for the string courses came from a variety of quite distant sources, up to 40–50 km from the town (Fig. 6.9). An arc of rock outcrops stretching north-east from Swindon to Oxford and beyond was the source of Portlandian calcareous sandstone and Coral Rag, while the Bargate Beds and the Hythe Beds of the western Weald to the east and south-east of the town were the source of the Lower Greensand. Malmstone (Upper Greensand), also originating from the western Weald, is also present, while the Plateau Gravels, nearer to the town at Finchampstead Ridges were the likely source of the ironstone. Chalk, from the same quarries that supplied the flint, would have been the main source of the lime putty used in the mortar along with locally available aggregates of sand and flint

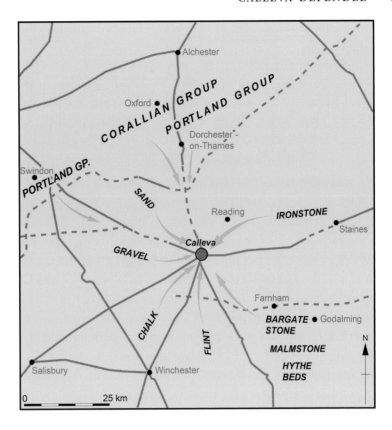

FIGURE 6.9 Map showing the locations of the source areas of the stone used in the construction of the city wall

gravel which bound the wall together. No deep trench was dug for its foundations, rather the wall sits on a shallow bed of gravel or, where it runs over soft or marshy ground, on oak piles.

How all the materials were brought to the town is uncertain, but the majority of our stone sources have outcrops which lie fairly close to the main Roman roads leading to Calleva. Transport in carts by road seems more likely than by river. The latter would have involved the multiple handling of loads, requiring them to be taken first from the quarry to a river such as the Kennet or Thames and then off-loading them from rafts or barges back on to carts for the last stretch to the town from the Loddon or Kennet, the nearest rivers to the town. Given the locations of the sources of the stone chosen for use in the wall, all the major roads could have been used. Since the maximum load for a cart was about 500 kg, somewhere in the region of about 200,000 wagon loads would have been needed to complete the task, of which almost a quarter, some 45,000 loads, would have been needed to cart the bonding stone. Obtaining a sufficient number of carts and oxen to pull them would have been another logistical difficulty for the builders to overcome, as would the feeding of the various labour forces and the beasts pulling the carts.

Why then, when clay and suitable timber for firing the kilns were locally available, were bricks not used in the string courses, as we see in the town walls of neighbouring London and Verulamium? Had the town lost the skills to make and fire bricks? If not, was there sufficient capacity to produce the quantities of brick required? That the production of brick and tile may have ceased or significantly declined by the late 3rd century is implied by the use of stone tile, rather than the familiar ceramic tegula and imbrex, for roofing in the town in the late Roman period. Exactly when this change took place is not known nor whether it was total or merely a change in emphasis towards a greater use of stone tile. Another factor affecting production was seasonality. Whereas brick making needed to avoid the wet and frosty winter and so was very largely confined to the months between April and October, stone could be quarried by unskilled labourers and carted throughout the year, even if actual construction work only took place over the spring to autumn period. If there was some urgency to complete the wall, it is possible that using stone throughout the build was seen as the more efficient way of achieving completion in the shortest possible time. The risks were spread among a number of labour forces: those working the various quarries, those involved in the transportation of materials from each quarry, those preparing the lime and those on site building the wall. Analysis of the way the wall was built suggests that three or four gangs may have worked simultaneously on different stretches of the wall, for example, one working west from the South Gate, another to the east and so on.

What prompted this enormous project, the greatest in the entire life of the town, and who paid for it? Although it is attractive to see the wall as simply an upgrade of a decaying earlier defence, the decision to build it would have lain with the imperial authorities who would also have had access to the resources at the scale required to build it, even if the civitas of the Atrebates was expected to repay all or some of the cost over the longer term. With no tradition in the town of building on this scale, central authority would also have provided the architect or engineer, probably drawn from the military, to be responsible for the project. The initiative may have been the Emperor Probus's (AD 276–282) who was active in the north-western provinces, strengthening frontier defences and restoring towns during his reign.

Although other towns in Britain were similarly defended around this time, Silchester's town wall stands out for the exceptional way it drew upon multiple, distant sources of stone for its bonding or levelling courses. It was not unusual for towns and forts to utilise stone from quarries accessible by sea, and thus cheaper to transport than by road, particularly where local stone was unavailable, as in the case of the walls of London, which used Kentish Rag imported via the Medway and Thames in conjunction with bonding courses of more local brick. We can only speculate whether the decision to use stone rather than brick at land-locked Silchester was a practical one, brought about by the absence of a sufficiently skilled work force to make tile, either at all, or in sufficient quantities to feed the building programme in a timely fashion, or whether there was a conscious, political decision to exploit resources which reached right to, or even beyond the margins of the civitas of the Atrebates, thus emphasising the extraordinary, prestigious nature of the project and endow the town with great status. If the latter, then the likely candidates as sponsors would be the usurper emperors of Britain, Carausius (286–293) and Allectus (293–296). Curiously and coincidentally, Silchester is the only town in Britain where there is a record of a find of a gold aureus – very rare finds indeed – of both Carausius and Allectus (Fig. 6.10).

One other piece of evidence may connect the usurper emperors with Calleva: both struck coin from a so far unidentified mint denoted as 'C' on the reverse of their coins. Camulodunum (Colchester) and Glevum (Gloucester), both coloniae, have been suggested as possible candidates, while Corinium (Cirencester), later to become a provincial capital, could be another. With its quite exceptional – and costly – city wall, whose construction could well have been initiated by Carausius, why not Calleva? When Rome had gathered its resources to re-take Britain, one

FIGURE 6.10 Gold aureus of usurper Emperor Allectus (293–296)
(COURTESY ROGER BLAND)

of the invading forces landed on the south coast in 296, somewhere near Southampton Water and it has been suggested that the battle which saw the end of Allectus took place near Silchester. The possible location is linked to the find of a large hoard of almost 30,000 coins, the latest of which date to 295–6, which was found not far away at Blackmoor in north Hampshire. If Calleva, along with London, the destination of the second invading force under Constantius Chlorus, were strongholds of the usurpers, it would have made good sense for each to have been a key target of one of the invading armies, hence, in Silchester's case, a landing on the south coast. That there may have been other consequences from this connection, however tentative this idea may be, with the usurpers will be explored further below.

## More changes

The late 3rd century saw other major changes affecting the organisation of the town as well as individual public and private buildings. First, the amphitheatre, which was extensively re-furbished with its entrance passages, arena wall and opposing recesses re-built in stone in the 3rd century (Figs 6.11–6.13). Lack of evidence makes dating this development difficult but one clue lies in the choice of stone rather than brick to serve as the bonding courses of the otherwise flint wall. This recalls the similar usage in the town wall but, whereas the latter contains a wide variety of stone types from sources 40–50 km distant from the town, the stone in the arena wall is predominantly of a brown, iron-oxide cemented sandstone of local origin. This might suggest the work on the amphitheatre was earlier than the building of the town wall and one possible context for it might have been a visit to the town by the Emperor Septimius Severus and his sons Caracalla and Geta when they were in Britain to lead the campaigns against the northern British tribes in 208–211. Any visit to the west from London, perhaps to inspect the legionary garrison at Caerleon, would have involved passing through and very probably staying in Calleva. However, for bonding courses to use stone rather than brick as early as the first years of the 3rd century requires further proof. An alternative context may have been the celebration of the 1000th anniversary of the founding of Rome in 248, extravagantly marked in the capital city by the Emperor Philip I. Perhaps a complete coincidence, but a coin of Philip, otherwise a rare find from Silchester, was found in the arena silts.

Significant change is also evident at the forum basilica where the

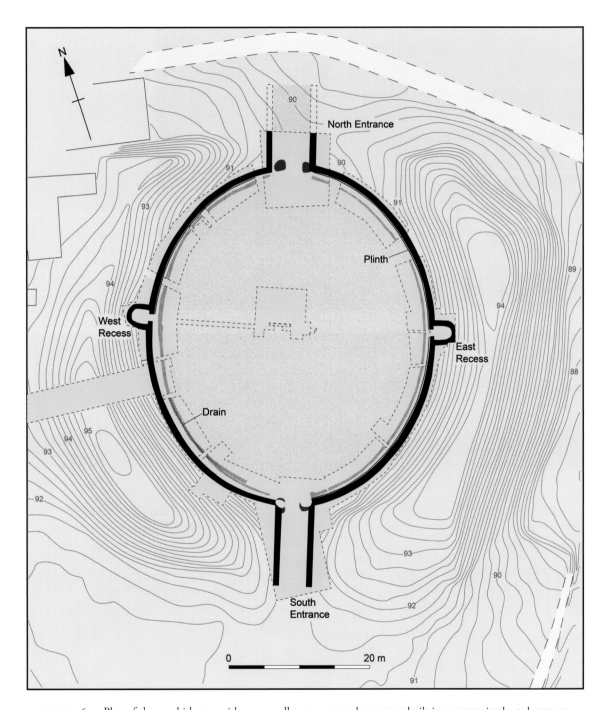

FIGURE 6.11 Plan of the amphitheatre with arena wall, entrances and recesses rebuilt in masonry in the 3rd century

FIGURE 6.12 View of the recess on the west side of the arena

FIGURE 6.13 Reconstruction showing the amphitheatre in use in the 3rd century by Peter Urmston
(© HISTORIC ENGLAND ARCHIVE)

0 1 2 3 4 5 cm

FIGURE 6.14 Fragment of mould of Bath stone from the forum basilica for making pewter tableware

great hall, the basilica itself, was given over to metalworking from the late 3rd century. While the antiquarian excavations of Joyce and the Society of Antiquaries had removed most of the remains of the occupation within the basilica, sufficient survived to attempt a characterisation. Most apparent was a range of metalworking practices. Bronze statuary was cut up and melted down, tableware of pewter (an alloy of tin and lead) was cast in moulds made from Bath stone (Fig. 6.14) and iron was both smelted from ore and forged into artefacts. There was also a lead mould for producing coins of the Gallic Emperor, Tetricus II, Caesar in 273–274, the young son of the Gallic Emperor Tetricus I (271–274). These activities took place alongside feasting, best illustrated by pits in a room at the north end of the hall, which contained a high proportion (up to 40%) of the bone of domestic fowl, especially cockerel, along with the remains of the main domesticates as well as marine fish and oyster. The high proportion of cockerel is interesting and two complementary interpretations suggest themselves: the birds may represent the remains of cockfighting or of sacrifices associated with the conduct of official rituals within this public building. Also, within the hall at its northern end, an area with a tiled floor was reserved for activities which resulted in a high incidence of coin loss from the late 3rd century onwards. Was this an area where taxes were received or was it connected with transactions, such as the purchase of pewter ware, relating to the metalworking in the adjacent space? Although we have little comparative evidence from elsewhere for how this type of public building might have been used in the late 3rd and 4th centuries, the mixture of high status activities exemplified by the feasting debris, cock fighting and dirty, malodorous metalworking is interesting.

Insula IX also shows major change in the late 3rd century (Figs 6.15–6.16). The big town house on the north-east to south-west alignment was demolished allowing for the re-organisation of space within the insula with a new, east–west property boundary bisecting the foundations of the old house. At least

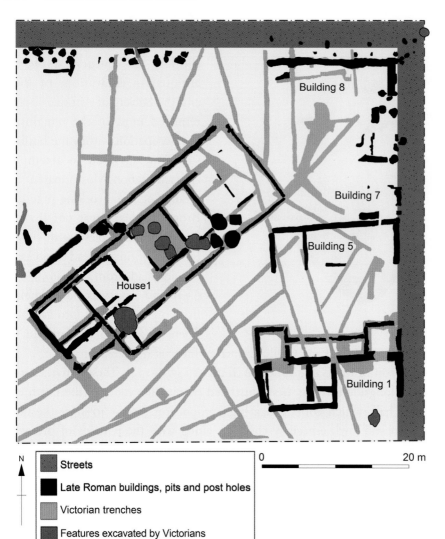

N

Streets

Late Roman buildings, pits and post holes

Victorian trenches

Features excavated by Victorians

0    20 m

FIGURE 6.15 Insula IX: plan of the excavated area in the late 3rd and 4th centuries

three new properties were discovered within the excavated area fronting on to the main north–south street, while two new builds have been identified by aerial photography on the west side of the block, the boundary between their properties coming somewhere in the middle. The radical nature of the change is illustrated by the fate of two robust, oak-lined wells in the south-east corner of the excavated area; constructed in the early 3rd century and potentially still serviceable, they were abandoned and backfilled. A new cottage was built in this south-east corner, its property impinging on the town house occupying the centre of the insula. This, too, was built on the north-east/ south-west, north-west/south-east orientation and, judging by the fragmented plan recovered by the antiquarian excavators, was likewise demolished. The

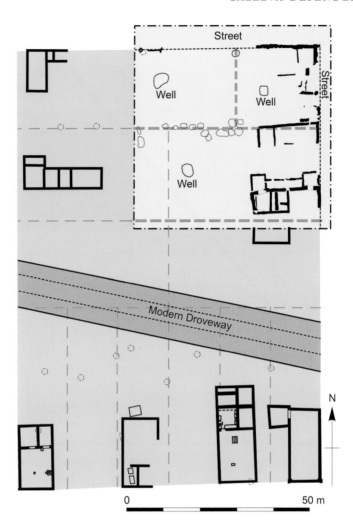

FIGURE 6.16 Insula IX: reconstructed plan of the whole insula in the late 3rd and 4th century

properties fronting onto the main east–west street presumably continued in use, perhaps with extended plots running back towards the middle of the block. All the property divisions of the block were now organised north–south/east–west, breaking arrangements which were originally established with the first settlement of Calleva at the end of the 1st century BC.

The loss of town houses leaving only commercial premises or small artisans' cottages fronting on to the streets can be paralleled elsewhere across the town. In the block, Insula XXVI, immediately to the north of Insula IX, there is another town house, also on the north-east to south-west orientation, whose remains were reported by Joyce as poorly preserved, itself suggestive of demolition. More emphatically, an adjacent, similarly aligned

house, appears to have been replaced by one or two strip buildings fronting on to, and at right-angles to, the street, while, on the west side of this insula, a small cottage, aligned with the street, appears to overlie the remains of another two small buildings on a north-east to south-west orientation. It seems, then, that Insula XXVI could also have been re-designed with all its properties aligned with the street grid. Without town houses, both insulae complement the remaining blocks in the north-west quadrant of the town which only ever appear to have been occupied by small cottages or commercial premises (Fig. 6.17).

In the centre of the town in Insula III, next to the forum basilica, we have already seen that the only substantial building recorded by the antiquarian excavations was an unfinished, early Roman town house. All the other buildings discovered or re-examined by the excavations of 2013–2016 proved to be the remains of late 3rd and 4th century cottages or strip buildings, the best preserved on the south side of the block. All are aligned with the grid. Further south in Insulas VIII, XVI and XVII, the early excavators found

FIGURE 6.17 Late Roman Insula IX in the wider context of the north-west quadrant and the insulae immediately east of the main north–south street of the Roman city. Buildings certainly or probably occupied in the 4th century in black; buildings certainly or probably abandoned before AD 300 in grey

more buildings where they were not able to recover their complete plans. Without exception these buildings were also on north-east to south-west or north-west to south-east alignments but, unlike the situation in the north-west of the town, they are found in insulae where there are other town houses or, in the case of Insula VIII, also the mansio. There is no obvious evidence in these southern blocks of radical re-planning or replacement with commercial premises or artisans' cottages.

Without a great deal more excavation we cannot be certain whether all the buildings with orientations askew to that of the street grid were abandoned and demolished at the same time, but the radical re-planning as well as demolition of town houses in Insulas IX and XXVI in the north-west quadrant suggests a single owner of each and, perhaps, the same owner of both. Was this a private individual or could the town itself have owned these and perhaps all the other insulae in the north-west quadrant which had no associated town house? Or, given the connection proposed above with the usurper emperors, were these confiscations by Constantius Chlorus of properties owned by supporters of Allectus? Whatever might be the case, no new town house was built, the owner living elsewhere but continuing to derive income from rent. In the case of municipal ownership, the income from sale or, more likely, rent from the properties, would have been available to support the public facilities of the town. It is intriguing that the affected insulae are those with houses on alignments quite different to that of the street grid, but we can only speculate as to the reason for this. Had long-established families living on these insulae finally died out? Did long established households need to increase their income by making more of their estate available to rent? Confiscations? Or a new order in the town finally demanding compliance with the street grid established some 200 years earlier? If this were the case, the new order appears to be implicitly or overtly attacking families which could trace ownership of their plots back to the earliest days of the settlement.

There is a parallel between the development of artisanal activity evident in the cottage and strip buildings constructed in Insula IX and the development of metalworking in the forum basilica. Indeed, in the later 3rd and 4th century iron working, both smelting and smithing, becomes a much more significant activity in Insula IX than ever before. It remains to be established whether iron working was also a feature of the occupation of other blocks of the town where late Roman strip buildings and artisanal cottages are to be found. How life changed in the town in other respects in the 4th century is the subject of the next chapter.

# CHAPTER SEVEN

# Late Roman Calleva

..................................................................................................................................

In the previous chapter we saw that there were some significant changes to the town in the late 3rd century, of which the building of the massive town wall was the most obvious and the most demanding on resources. But did a development like this have much effect on day-to-day living in the life of the town? Although the materials for the wall were drawn from far afield, the spend on feeding the builders and from whatever was left of the wage they were given surely had an impact on the economy of the town during the lifetime of the project. Low value copper alloy coins circulated in considerable numbers across southern Britain during the period of construction between the AD 260s and 290s, and they have been found in all but the very small, recent excavations within the town. Even if the purchasing power of a single coin was negligible, collectively such coin could have made a difference. But once the big capital project was completed, did life revert to how it was and not otherwise change much through the 4th century?

What was new after the completion of the town wall? There were no new public buildings and, as far as we know, the town still lacked a theatre. If we regard temples as public buildings, then we cannot be sure that there were no new dedications since only one, other than the possible church (see below), has been explored by modern methods within the town. The public baths were almost 200 years old by the end of the 3rd century and it is not surprising that there is evidence of re-furbishment and alteration. Around the turn of the 3rd and 4th centuries an extension was built to replace the existing, but ageing, tepidarium on the west side of the building, its furnace located in the ruins of its predecessor (Fig. 7.1). A century later, around the turn of the 4th and 5th centuries, another new tepidarium was built to

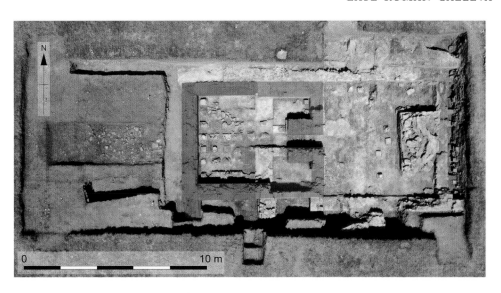

FIGURE 7.1 New tepidarium (warm room) added on the west side of the public baths in the late 3rd/ early 4th century. The furnace was operated within the shell of the abandoned earlier tepidarium

replace an equivalent on the east side of the building (Fig. 8.1). Even if the original building lost some of its integrity, the baths clearly remained an important part of the life of the town throughout its later life.

If we look across the plan of the town we can only guess at how many of the houses and commercial premises were occupied through the 4th century, since all we have from the antiquarian excavations are their plans and a brief description of them: there is no information about their date. However, since we believe that the buildings with incomplete or fragmentary plans are likely to have been demolished before the end of the 3rd century (Chapter 6), it is a reasonable assumption that all the remaining buildings, those where the early excavators were confident of the plans they made, were standing and occupied during the 4th century. To add to this we have the evidence of mosaics where, even if there is no independent evidence of date, the style may indicate they are late Roman. This topic will be pursued further below. The design of hypocausts changes in the 3rd and 4th centuries from a total reliance on columns of bricks (pilae) to support the floor to either a combination of pilae and otherwise solid foundations cut by channels (composite) (Fig. 8.1) for the hot air to circulate through or just the latter style (channeled type where the hot air passed along narrow channels radiating out from the furnace between the masses of masonry supporting the floor). Houses furnished with the late types are widely distributed across the town. Further, and more certain, but relatively few in number, we have the buildings dated by modern excavations to the late 3rd or 4th century.

# A church?

The first, and the most problematic building to consider is the possible church which was first discovered in 1892 and then re-excavated in 1961 by Sir Ian Richmond and George Boon (Figs 1.15; 7.2). Because of its potential significance, it is worth considering in some detail. It is located just to the south-east of the forum in Insula IV, the central insula of the town, and its plan shares many of the characteristics of a Christian church: it has a nave flanked by aisles which widen towards the west end to form lateral chambers or quasi-transepts, and it is closed by an apse at the west end. At the east end is a vestibule or, if described in terms of a church, a narthex, the place for those not eligible for admission to the general congregation. The whole building is small, only 13 × 9 m overall, with walls 0.6 m thick. It is built of flint with brick quoins and the floor of the nave and the apse was covered (tessellated) with cubes of red brick. In addition, the apse was decorated with a panel of geometric mosaic, 1.52 m square (Fig. 7.3). Stephen Cosh and David Neal describe it thus:

> The square centre piece is an adapted black-and-white chequered scheme in which some small squares are replaced with the opposite colour to produce four chequered squares with alternately shaded L-shapes in the corners. This panel is surrounded by a band of tangent-poised squares, alternately red and grey, flanked by black triple fillets. Between the inner black line and the chequered design is a simple dotted fillet in black and white.

They compare it with mosaics from Verulamium (St Albans), Gloucester, Leicester and Wroxeter, all except the first dated to the mid-to-later 2nd century. Although the excavator of the Verulamium mosaic thought it was laid at the end of 3rd century, there was no supporting evidence for such a date. Stylistically, then, the mosaic could be late 2nd century but what distinguishes it from the others listed above, and may have Christian significance, is that the four alternating black-on-white and white-on-black chequered squares create a central cruciform element in the design.

The late 2nd century is also the date of the latest sherd of pottery found stratified beneath the building. Two sherds of pottery, one of a similar date, the other late 2nd or early 3rd, were also found in the floor and drain of a timber building which must have preceded the construction of the 'church'. Put together all this evidence this would indicate a date after AD 200 for its construction. But this is a long way from the time when Christianity

FIGURE 7.2 Plan of
the possible church
in Insula IV after the
re-excavation by Sir Ian
Richmond in 1961

| | | |
|---|---|---|
| Wall / Flints | Mortar | Red tessera / Tile |
| Gravel | Hearth | Post-hole |
| Hollow | Plough scar | Victorian pit |

FIGURE 7.3 Mosaic from the apse of the possible church (courtesy Stephen Cosh and David Neal, by permission of the Society of Antiquaries)

became the official religion of the Roman Empire after the Edict of Milan issued in 313.

To the east of the building and on the same axis is a tile base 1.22 m square set in the middle of a flint foundation. The surviving straight edge on the south side suggested that this was the floor of a small building, some 3.5 m square, though no other evidence was found to strengthen the case that it was enclosed. In its west end was a flint and tile-lined pit or soakaway, 0.5 m square and 1.0 m deep. Although this has variously been interpreted as a baptistery or laver with an associated soakaway, there are difficulties with such interpretations. First, as a baptistery it would be expected at this early date that the baptismal basin would have been sunk below ground level and entered by steps, since the rite was by immersion. Although the lack of evidence for a surrounding building has been a problem for some, the straight edge on one side of the flint foundation could have been created by a sleeper beam resting against it, in which case one could envisage a small wooden building resting on sleeper beams, its east side very close to the west end of the church. An alternative interpretation sees the tile base as support for a laver, rather than a baptismal basin, where worshippers could wash their hands and face before entering the church. One other possibility has also been entertained: that the structure is not Christian at all but the basis for a pagan altar.

In deciding whether or not the building was a church we are left with a plan which, with its lateral chambers or 'quasi-transepts', is difficult to parallel in a non-Christian building. Otherwise, the form and size of the building is not dissimilar to that of pagan mystery temples like, for example, the mithraeum in London. At Silchester, there is a parallel in Insula XXI where a small (7.5 × 5.8 m) building, oriented north–south with an apse at the north end, fronts on to the main east–west street at the south-east corner of the block. The orientation and lateral entrance argue against it being a church but it has been suggested that it was a 'schola', or meeting place of guild.

There were no finds of a Christian character from the 'church' in Insula IV (and few from the town as a whole), but the cruciform element in the centre of the mosaic may have had Christian significance, although the closest parallels to the design are dated to the later 2nd century. While coin finds from within the building show use up to around the mid-4th century, there is still a question about the date of its construction. On present evidence this looks to be 3rd rather than (early) 4th century. Though it is unclear how many and how much of the deposits which pre-date its construction still survive, it is likely that only removing the rest of the tessellated floor has the potential to produce more excavated evidence which might refine the date.

## Town houses

Determination of the date, function and character of the occupation of particular buildings is not a problem which is solely confined to the possible church. The great majority of buildings revealed by the antiquarian excavations lack any chronology; dated buildings are the exception. How then, without much more excavation, can we begin to gain insight into the character of the 4th century town? Houses with mosaic floors offer a possible way forward. As we saw with the situation in the 2nd century at

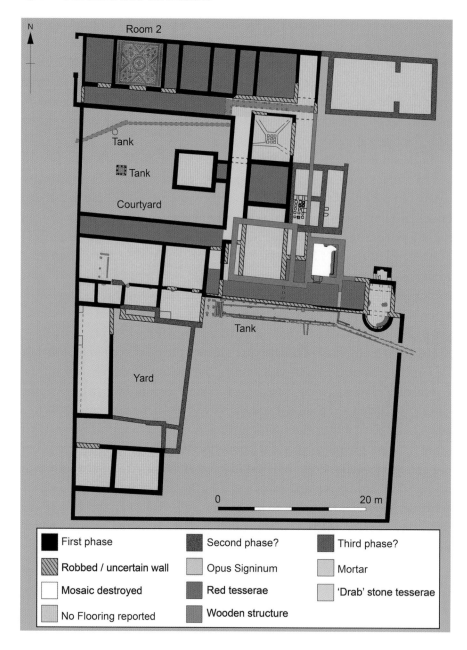

N

Room 2

Tank

Tank

Courtyard

Tank

Yard

0                    20 m

| First phase | | Second phase? | | Third phase? |
|---|---|---|---|---|
| Robbed / uncertain wall | | Opus Signinum | | Mortar |
| Mosaic destroyed | | Red tesserae | | 'Drab' stone tesserae |
| No Flooring reported | | Wooden structure | | |

FIGURE 7.4 Insula XXXIV: plan of House 1, showing the location of the 4th century mosaic

Silchester, excavation elsewhere across Britain has given us a framework for understanding the development of mosaic art in the province. This study of all the known pavements or fragments of pavements has given us an indication of which floors at Silchester are likely to be 4th century. Even if not all the parts of the buildings in question were necessarily occupied in the 4th century, this stylistic approach gives us a start. For example,

FIGURE 7.5 Insula
XXXIV House 1:
digital reconstruction
of 4th century mosaic
in Room 2, re-laid in
Stratfield Saye House
(courtesy Stephen
Cosh and David Neal,
by permission of the
Society of Antiquaries)

the house which occupies the north-west quarter of Insula XXXIV has
a geometrically patterned mosaic, its design a saltire, formed by triangles
midway along each side (Figs 7.4–7.5). It recalls mosaics which have been
assigned to a workshop centred on Cirencester, called the 'Saltire Group',
that is dated approximately to the mid-4th century. It decorated a room in
the north range which runs parallel with the street leading from the forum
to the temple quarter. There were other rooms in the house, particularly in
the east range, which show evidence of substantial alteration, likely to be 4th
century in date, but an associated mosaic was almost entirely lost. There is
a further courtyard to the south with possible work rooms along the street
side. This is a large house, also with a composite hypocaust, and all of it is
likely to have been occupied in the 4th century, but only fresh excavation
has a chance to demonstrate whether this is the case.

House 1, in the north-west corner of Insula XXVII, also has pavements
which are assigned to the 4th century (Fig. 7.6–7.8). One of these, a fragment
of one corner, depicts the bust of a female figure. She has red flowers in
her hair and wears a grey cloak, while over her left shoulder is a twig-like

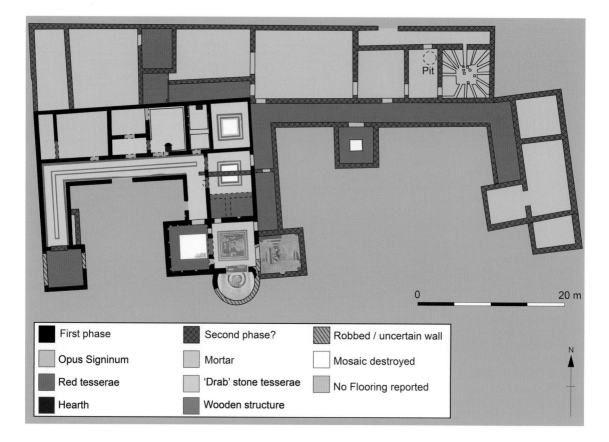

First phase

Opus Signinum

Red tesserae

Hearth

Second phase?

Mortar

'Drab' stone tesserae

Wooden structure

Robbed / uncertain wall

Mosaic destroyed

No Flooring reported

object. The flowers suggest identification with one of the seasons, probably Summer, the other corners of the mosaic occupied by Spring, Autumn and Winter (Fig. 7.8). This, too, is a large house, also with composite hypocausts, occupying almost the full width of the block, and with a second courtyard on the east side. It seems likely, but only further excavation will determine this, that the entirety was occupied in the 4th century.

Earlier, we described one of the two large houses which between them took up the entirety of Insula XIV. While both houses were almost certainly occupied through the 4th century, the mosaic panels decorating the gallery linking the west and east wings of the second house have close parallels with 4th century mosaics in the south of England (Fig. 7.9). Most of the rooms of the north and west residential ranges were furnished with mosaics, one attributed to the 2nd century, the others poorly preserved and of uncertain date. Like its neighbour, all of the house is likely to have been in use and occupied in the 4th century, and both have composite hypocausts.

FIGURE 7.6 Insula XXVII: plan of House 1

FIGURE 7.8  Insula XXVII House 1: detail of a
4th century mosaic, showing one of the seasons,
probably Summer

(COURTESY STEPHEN COSH AND DAVID NEAL, BY PERMISSION OF
THE SOCIETY OF ANTIQUARIES)

FIGURE 7.7  Insula XXVII House 1: 4th century mosaic

(COURTESY STEPHEN COSH AND DAVID NEAL, BY PERMISSION OF THE SOCIETY OF ANTIQUARIES)

FIGURE 7.9  Insula XIV
House 2: probable 4th
century gallery mosaics
(COURTESY STEPHEN COSH AND
DAVID NEAL, BY PERMISSION OF
THE SOCIETY OF ANTIQUARIES)

# Smaller buildings

At the other end of the scale are the remains of humbler buildings, identified as shops, workshops and artisans' cottages, which have been investigated by modern excavation in Insula III and Insula IX and dated to the late 3rd and 4th centuries. Taking Insula IX first, and going from south to north, we have first a small cottage, end on to the north–south street, with its entrance on the north side (see Fig. 6.15, Fig. 7.10). Originally a simple building (17.5 × 5.0 m) of perhaps just two main rooms, it was aggrandised by the addition of a corridor flanked by two projecting 'tower' rooms on the north side. A coin of the usurper emperor, Carausius (286–93), from a rubbish pit cut by the foundations tells us that the original building cannot be earlier than AD 286, but there is only less closely datable pottery to indicate an early 4th century for the later additions.

The 'grand' side of the building looked across to a smaller, two-roomed shop or workshop, only 18 × 6 m, and also built end-on to the street. Except for the foundations for the wall which fronted on to the street, its remains were not substantial and almost no trace could be found of foundations for a southern wall. No internal floor surfaces survived. As for date, the foundations cut through deposits which contained 4th century pottery. It seems very likely that both buildings, each looking across a gravel yard to the other, belonged to the same property with its northern boundary running west along the line of the north wall of the northern building. Whereas the larger building almost certainly had an upper storey, its plan revealing a small internal space which could have accommodated a staircase, the lesser building almost certainly did not. The larger building seems to have been of part flint, part timber-frame construction with a roof of stone tiles, the smaller solely of timber frame, perhaps with a thatched roof.

A feature of both these buildings is that their foundation trenches, where

FIGURE 7.10 Insula
IX: reconstructed view
looking north along the
main north–south street
(BY MARGARET MATHEWS)

they survived, were filled with gravel, not flint as had been used earlier in the 2nd century. Such buildings would have been invisible to the antiquarian excavators, unless courses of flint above the foundations still survived the hundreds of years of ploughing which have truncated the latest occupation of the town. Although the buildings had been cut by exploratory trenches in 1893, they were not recognised for what they were. In the case of the larger cottage, only the projecting 'tower' rooms and linking corridor were recognised, but not the remainder of the building where no courses of flint survived (see Fig. 1.22). Missing the buildings constructed with similar foundations recalls the inability of the antiquarian excavators to recover the remains of timber buildings typical of the early Roman period.

The difficulties of building recognition become much more acute as we continue north along the north–south street to the end of the insula. There, at the corner and close to the east–west street, was an area of reddened clay and tile, the unmistakeable remains of a long-lived hearth. Tracing the building which enclosed it – assuming that it was, indeed, roofed over – proved extremely difficult. Slight evidence in the form of a mix of post-holes and a shallow foundation cut for a north and east wall were found. There was no indication of the other two walls but a maximum extent to the west and south is arguably determined by the location of a contemporary well, which was probably sited outside the building. To conclude, we envisage a building of timber-frame construction which rested on the ground surface without substantial foundations but whose exact ground plan we struggled to establish with any certainty.

Just as challenging are the remains of one other structure between the corner building and the two-roomed shop or workshop to the south. The walls of what seems to have been no more than a very small hut, some 7.0 × 3.5 m, were defined by a combination of a shallow construction trench, which, like its neighbour, was most evident against the street, and flat stones to support posts. One implication of the discoveries in Insula IX is that the slighter buildings of late Roman Calleva are probably very under-represented in the 'Great Plan' of 1908. If there was little prospect of the early excavators recognising buildings where only gravel-filled foundations trenches remained, there was even less chance of their narrow, exploratory trenches picking up the even slighter buildings which we have proposed occupied part of the frontage of the north–south street in Insula IX.

Damage by the plough had a similar impact on the late Roman remains in Insula III as it had had in Insula IX. Excavations were undertaken in the north-west, north-east and south-east corners of the block in an attempt to characterise its occupation and test the extent of its early development as much as the nature of its occupation in the later 3rd and 4th centuries. Excavation in all three areas produced remains reminiscent of what had been found in Insula IX, particularly of buildings resting on gravel-filled construction trenches (Fig. 7.11).

In the middle of the south side of the block were the remains of a cottage similar in plan to the one excavated in Insula IX and, like its counterpart, also built end-on to the street, its frontage with its distinctive 'tower' rooms facing east. Although built on gravel-filled foundations, the lowest flint courses survived well enough for it to have been discovered in 1891 and the 2016 excavation confirmed its late Roman date. It was a different situation in the north-west corner where excavation confirmed a building (15 × 7 m) which had been identified by geophysics, but not by the excavation of 1891. Here no flint coursing survived, only the gravel-filled foundation trenches. Next to it, running along the edge of the east–west street were post-holes which probably represent the frontage of another building but one whose full plan could not be traced. This recalls both the north-east and south-

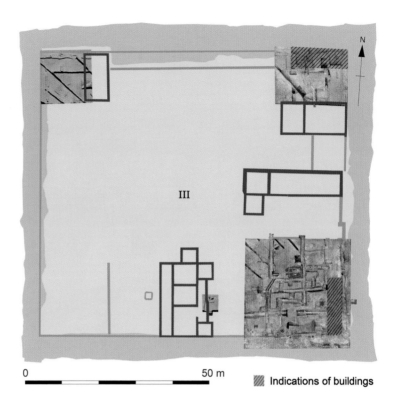

FIGURE 7.11 Insula III: plan of the late Roman occupation

0       50 m

▨ Indications of buildings

east corners of the insula where almost all but the frontages of late Roman buildings had been destroyed by extensive antiquarian excavation. An unusual late Roman structure in the south-east corner was a small standalone corn-dryer (Fig. 7.12). Finally, excavation in advance of the building of an extension on the south side of St Mary's church revealed a little more of the small house or cottage first discovered in 1890. This, too, is reminiscent in its plan of the cottages in Insulas III and IX, and also proved to be of late Roman date.

What do these discoveries tell us about the state of the town in the 4th century? Modern excavation in Insulas III and IX has added several buildings which were not recognised as such by the antiquarian excavators to the plan of the town and confirmed their late 3rd or 4th century date. Geophysics has shown that many previously unrecognised buildings exist right across the town and that there were also unrecognised extensions to buildings, such as some of the larger town houses revealed by the antiquarian excavations. The reasons why these remains were not picked up by the systematic trial-trenching of the Society of Antiquaries' project is unclear. The most likely explanations are that either only the gravel-filled foundation trenches typical

FIGURE 7.12 Insula III:
probable corn-drying
oven

of late Roman building survived or that the remains of masonry buildings
that had been abandoned or demolished before the late 3rd or 4th century
were so slight, or so badly robbed of their re-usable stonework, that they
escaped detection. Generalising a little from what has been observed in
Insulas IX and XXVI, we can suggest that structures which had been re-

built in masonry or built anew in the 2nd century on orientations which did not align with the street grid, were probably abandoned and demolished before the end of the 3rd century (see Fig. 6.17 and Chapter 6). There are exceptions, most notably House 2 in Insula XXIII which, by the integrity of its plan, looks to be a strong candidate for continuing in occupation in the 4th century. It also has a composite hypocaust.

On the other hand, buildings whose plans do align with the street grid are more likely to have been occupied in the late 3rd or 4th century; some may have been newly built, but this was almost certainly not the case with the larger town houses. We do not yet have an example of a masonry-founded structure, large or small, which was aligned with the street grid and with evidence of abandonment and demolition before the end of the 3rd century. Only fresh excavation can resolve these questions of date. And only excavation, not aerial photography or geophysics, can identify buildings, like those in the north-east corner of Insula IX, or around Insula III, which were either constructed solely of timber or are represented only by fragments of their frontages or ground plan.

The late Roman town was certainly flourishing through the 4th century, but we are not in a position yet to say whether it was more or less successful then than in the 1st or 2nd century. Only the excavation in Insula IX has systematically explored the earlier Roman occupation, and this has been sufficient to show that there were, as long suspected, buildings of timber frame construction alongside those with masonry foundations. This is very likely to have been the situation across the town. A possible indicator of changing population numbers might be the incidence of wells within the town, but we only have a complete picture from part of Insula IX. However, given that the number there in the 2nd century was more or less the same as in the 4th, there would appear to have been no significant change in the number of residents in the insula. Whether this was the case across the town remains to be established, but, as has been remarked before, since there was no change in the area of town defended between the end of the 2nd and late 3rd century, population numbers probably remained static.

CHAPTER EIGHT

# Living in late Roman Calleva

....................................................................................................

At the beginning of the 4th century, the Roman conquest of southern Britain, some two and a half centuries earlier, might have seemed like ancient history. What might once have still seemed to Britons like new practices and behaviours two or three generations on at the beginning of the early 2nd century had probably become firmly established and widely accepted across the province by the end of it. How much, if at all, did daily life change another 100 years on, at the beginning of the 4th century?

There are some obvious continuities, typically to be seen among the wealthier inhabitants of the town in the continued development of private housing and its decoration. Painted wall plasters and mosaic or otherwise patterned floors were still favoured; suites of rooms in the larger houses continued to be heated by hypocausts. On the other hand, and as previously, private bath houses were not built, reliance continuing to be placed on the public baths. Evidence of their popularity can be seen in the repairs and alterations made to them through the 4th century (Fig. 8.1). We can only speculate whether individuals within the town were also allowed to access the only other baths, those attached to the mansio, alongside the travellers on official business.

## Food and drink

To help us reconstruct daily life in the 4th century recent excavation has given us some insight from both the investigation of public buildings, like the forum basilica and the baths, and the private world of the shops and workshops of Insula III, but especially a transformed Insula IX (Fig. 8.2).

FIGURE 8.1 A new tepidarium (warm room) with a composite hypocaust: a very late 4th century addition to the public baths. View to the east. The furnace was in the middle of the north side

Food is where our investigation should begin and Insula IX has provided us with a rich seam of information on the great variety of types of food consumed. Preservation by waterlogging, typically found at the bottom of wells, and by mineralisation, usually associated with cess pits, has greatly enriched the picture of the range of plant foods, fish, small birds and mammals, which were consumed. Much harder to ascertain is how frequently the different types of food were eaten, though the diet is likely to have continued to be dominated by cereals and meat from the major domesticates.

Thus, from the rubbish pits, cess pits and abandoned wells associated with the less affluent households of artisans and craftsmen in Insula IX we have an astonishing range of evidence: beef continued to be the main source of meat but it was accompanied in almost equal proportions by mutton and pork. The presence of the shoulder blades of cattle pierced to take metal hooks suggests that some of the beef was smoked. Domestic fowl were also eaten but with a predominance of adults and females, in other words only after their egg-laying days were over. Wild birds that were deliberately hunted for food included duck and woodcock. Wild animals were also eaten,

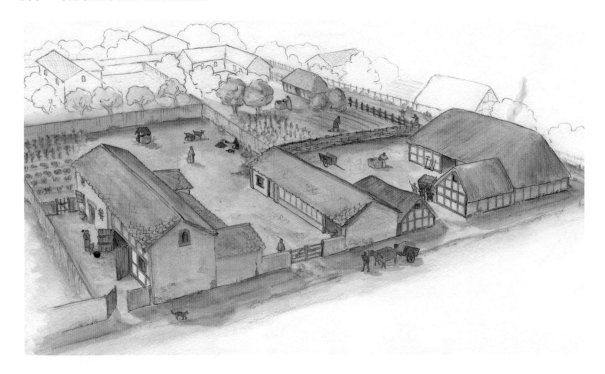

particularly roe and red deer and hare, as were freshwater and marine fish. The great majority of the fish bones recovered belonged to eel, but those of salmon, trout and pike as well as bass, sea bream, flatfish and smelt were also found. The small size of the fish raises the possibility that they derived from the much-favoured fish sauce (garum) made from decomposing fish. There was also a little oyster.

Spelt wheat and barley were the main cereals, supplemented by some lentils, field or Celtic beans and peas. Flavourings included coriander, celery seed, summer savory, opium poppy seed, mustard and, perhaps, dill. There was a rich fruit component to the diet with apples predominating, the quantity perhaps indicating the cultivated variety rather than the wild crab-apple. Other fruits likely to have been grown locally include plum, cherry and perhaps wild/alpine strawberry, while the occurrence of grape, fig and pickled cucumber point to exotic, but probably rare, imports. Hazelnuts and walnuts were eaten as were blackberries. The presence of the seeds of the poisonous hemlock is also interesting. With its capacity in small quantities to calm, it is presumed that it was used for medicinal purposes.

To add to the evidence of the imported fruits, there are also a few amphorae representing the importation of wine from Asia Minor, present-day Turkey, and olive-oil from north Africa, especially from what is now Tunisia.

FIGURE 8.2
Reconstructed view of the north-east part of Insula IX in the 4th century
(BY MARGARET MATHEWS)

If what has been found in Insula IX is typical of what working families consumed in the town, only further work will discover how different were the food types eaten by the richer households. It is likely that greater quantities of imported foodstuffs were consumed, including wine and olive-oil, as well as of rarer, local foods, such as marine fish and oysters, and hunted wild animals including birds. Although we do not have the conditions of waterlogging and mineralisation that were present in Insula IX from other modern excavations within the town, we can see some differences in the range and abundance of those food types which have been recovered. Late Roman deposits beside the North Gate, probably rubbish from the occupants of the adjacent town house in Insula XXIV, were dominated by the remains of cattle but, surprisingly, the remains of bird were as abundant as sheep/goat and pig. These were mostly domestic fowl, along with some geese and duck and wild birds, of which woodcock was the most common species. Both marine and freshwater fish were also present and oyster was abundant, the quantities markedly greater than those found in Insula IX.

In the case of the forum basilica the character of the food remains probably relates to some of the activities and rituals carried out in this public building. For example, the high incidence of adult male domestic fowl may reflect an association with sacrifice or cock fighting. Sacrifice may also be the explanation for the unusually high proportion of sheep compared with cattle, which otherwise typically dominate late Roman animal bone assemblages across the town. Overall, the late Roman assemblage from the forum basilica displays characteristics compatible with conspicuous consumption, probably following sacrifice and perhaps best evidenced by the very high proportion of bird bones, accounting for 40% of the animal bone from one large deposit. Some two-thirds of the birds were of domestic fowl but there was also domestic goose, duck and pigeon as well as several wild species of which the woodcock was the most abundant. Conspicuous, too, is the incidence of shellfish, mostly oyster, but also mussels and whelks. Of more than 2000 shells recovered, over 80% were oyster. Whereas the total amount of oyster from the 3000 m² of late Roman deposits at Insula IX amounted to the equivalent of no more than about a dozen whole oysters, the comparable figure from the limited and truncated deposits of the forum basilica was about 900, or about one shellfish fragment to three identifiable animal bones. To this we can add the consumption of fish: with conditions of mineralisation favouring the preservation of fish bone, especially eel, there were additionally some 43 bones of freshwater and marine fish from Insula IX. At 101 fish bones, the total from the surviving remains of the late Roman occupation of the forum basilica was more than twice the Insula IX figure. Other than the charred remains of cereals, the absence of waterlogged or mineralised deposits from the forum basilica means that it is not possible to characterise further the range of plant foods consumed there. A single sherd of North African amphora is the only indication of the consumption of olive-oil.

Looking back across these three excavations where there has been systematic study of surviving food remains, it would appear that a significant indicator of social status is variation in the abundance of oyster, minimally represented across the large excavated area of Insula IX, but abundant in the spatially limited late Roman deposits at the forum basilica and the North Gate (which probably equates with the nearby town house). The relative abundance of bird, both domestic and wild species, at the forum basilica and the North Gate also sets the public building and the town house apart from the artisanal nature of the occupation of Insula IX. Fish, especially marine species, also look to be important as a social discriminator. In Insula IX where the particular circumstances of mineralisation contributed to the preservation of fish bone, marine species were definitely in the minority compared with freshwater species, especially eel, while, with less favourable conditions of preservation, the opposite appears to be the case at the town house and the forum basilica. Judging by the rarity of cut or butchery marks, domestic animals – horse, dog and cat – were very rarely eaten, if at all, by some households.

## Breeding and growing

Following on from considering the consumption of food, evaluating the evidence for its provision in the town seems an obvious starting point for a consideration of the occupations of the inhabitants of late Roman Calleva. Although we cannot pinpoint precisely where in the town they were kept, domestic fowl, especially chicken, but also geese, duck and pigeon, were raised and the females kept, first for their eggs and then as a source of meat. The discovery of the foetal or neonate bones of pig and of sheep/goat indicates that they were raised in or very close to the town and the same may also be true of some cattle as the bones of very young animals have been recovered. As in the 1st century, milk production does not seem to have been important. Specific indications of domestic animals being penned or grazed within the town have been found in both Insula III and IX.

Micromorphological analysis of soils from Insula III has revealed evidence of animal dung from several 4th century contexts in the north-east corner close to the forum basilica, while in Insula IX there was the rare find of a mineralised goat dropping in a cess pit next to the cottage in the south-east corner of the excavated area. Also in that insula, the waterlogged seeds of wetland plants from a well deposit may have derived from the dung of domestic animals grazing on marshy pasture outside the town. It has also been suggested that the quality of the cereal remains from Insula IX was consistent with an interpretation as 'tailcorn' (small, sometimes poor quality grain), and so was suitable as animal fodder. All of this adds credence to earlier indications that, while lacking any specific evidence for how they were used, some of the buildings within the town served as barns, byres and granaries.

If some of the open spaces within the town were used as pasture, others probably served variously as horticultural plots or orchards. The incidence of the seeds of some of the flavourings commonly used in the preparation of food, such as coriander, celery, summer savory, poppy, mustard and, perhaps, dill strongly suggests cultivation in the town. So, too, the incidence of fruit, particularly apples, but also plum, cherry and perhaps wild/alpine strawberry, points to orchards within or close to the town.

However, despite a degree of local provision, it is unlikely that the town was self-sufficient in food. We have seen this specifically with the finds of probable or certain imports such as grape, fig and cucumber from Insula IX, although it is unlikely that these constituted more than a fraction of the plant-based foods consumed. Some cereals were grown locally as the pollen evidence suggests, and, besides the one in Insula III (Chapter 7), at least one other corn-drying oven has been found in the town. However, most of the grain probably came in from country estates. The virtual absence of querns for grinding corn into flour by hand suggests that milling took place elsewhere, either on estates outside the town or in dedicated mills within or close to the town. In acquiring flour rather than grain and thereby paying for the added value of the processing, this staple would have cost those inhabitants of Calleva without their own supplies a little more. Supplies of meat from the town or from its immediate neighbourhood are also likely not to have been sufficient. Some of the shortfall would have been made up by animals hunted locally (although hunting was an elite pastime), while the Kennet and Loddon are likely to have been the source of eel and freshwater fish. Otherwise, animals arrived in the town from neighbouring farms on the hoof, though some meat seems to have been supplied as joints, including smoked shoulders of beef. We do not know where the animals were butchered but the presence of all parts of the skeletons of the main domesticates in deposits across the town suggests that some butchery took place in the household, though larger animals, especially cattle, would have required specialist butchers.

What is very different from the situation in the first and second centuries is the scarcity of amphoras, the pottery jars which carried wine, olive-oil, fish sauce and other luxury foods from the Mediterranean world to the north-western provinces like Britain. Although we have noted the occasional finds of oil-carrying African amphorae and, in one instance, of a vessel from the region of modern Turkey, they are, as elsewhere across Britain, very rare. Nor do we have a late Roman example of an imported wooden barrel of the type which we believe carried wine in the 1st and 2nd centuries. Is this because this trade had also ceased or is it that we have not yet discovered a suitable environment of this period where such an item might have been preserved? In the past they had been used to line wells, but none of the late Roman wells so far discovered has revealed any trace of a lining. The latest wells with preserved linings are those of early 3rd century date from Insula IX, but these were made of oak boarding. It is hard to imagine barrels not being used in 4th century Britain, but if they were smaller and not so susceptible to re-use in environments where they might be preserved, they would be even less likely to survive in the archaeological record than their larger predecessors.

## Craft and industry

Suitably fed, how did the inhabitants spend their days? Here we must distinguish between those activities, like preparing and eating food, which cannot readily be evidenced in the archaeological record, and those that do leave a mark. Judging by the row of narrow-fronted properties competing for space either side of the main east–west street, traffic passing through the town generated a lot of business and some of this may have spread to premises up the side streets. In this sense the 4th century may have seen business as usual, with little or no change from previous centuries. However, there are two types of industry which do seem to be more prominent in the 4th century than earlier: metalworking and bone processing. We have already seen how the great hall of the forum basilica was devoted to metalworking with iron smelting and forging alongside the working of non-ferrous metals.

To give some idea of what was made, we can infer from the stone moulds which were found in the basilica that the manufacture of pewter tableware was one important activity (see Fig. 6.14). Pewter, made from an alloy of lead and tin, was popular in late Roman Britain and the association of its manufacture with Calleva's principal public building suggests that here it was controlled by the town's authorities. Clues to the types of iron artefact that were made in the basilica are given by the grooves worn into the pieces of stone roofing tiles used as makeshift whetstones. It is hard to match the size and profiles of the grooves with the range of iron items actually recovered from the basilica or reported from the town more widely, but they would have been used to finish or sharpen items such as daggers, knives and small cleavers, and perhaps also punches and chisels. Some of these items may have been sold to consumers outside the town.

Metal workers in Insula IX also used discarded roofing tiles as whetstones, but the wear patterns suggest a different range of activities to those carried out in the basilica. These might have included the finishing off or sharpening of small items such as knives, razors and surgical tools, while the finely grooved stones were perhaps used for items like needles, pins and styli. The waste from both smelting and smithing was distributed widely across the excavated area of Insula IX, suggesting that these activities were carried out by most, if not all the households, with a greater concentration at the cottage in the south-east corner.

It is tempting to think that all the items of iron recovered from the late Roman town were made there and it is possible – but impossible to prove – that this was the case. Two remarkable late Roman hoards of ironwork from the antiquarian excavations give insight into the range of iron tools potentially available in the town (Fig. 8.3). Over 100 items survive and these include collections of blacksmith's, carpenter's, as well as farrier's, shoemaker's and agricultural tools along with miscellaneous pieces such as the pivot for a mill-stone, a linch-pin from a vehicle's wheel, a sword blade, cauldron chains, a large padlock and a cook's gridiron; the latter is elaborately constructed and has been described as a smith's *tour de force*. Since some of the items are incomplete or broken, it seems possible that the two collections belonged to blacksmiths who had stored scraps for recycling along with their finished products. The pits in which the objects were placed are about 140 m apart, one in Insula I, bordering on the main east–west street, the other in Insula XXIII, close to the North Gate. It would be fascinating to re-excavate the context and general environs in which these hoards of ironwork were found to see whether they were located in

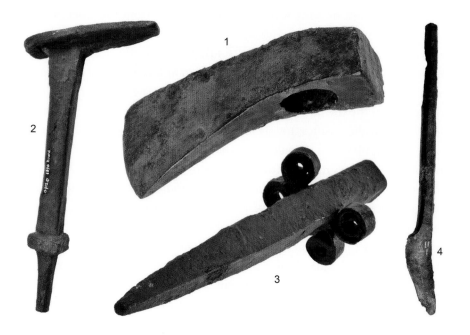

FIGURE 8.3 Tools from the hoards of ironwork from late Roman Calleva: 1: axe head; 2: cobbler's last; 3: field anvil; 4: plough coulter

areas where much iron working took place. But, as we shall see in the next chapter, these collections are likely to have been deposited in the dying days of the town and may have been brought in from the countryside to what was perceived as a secure place and subsequently concealed in the pits where they were found. They therefore may have nothing to do with iron working or the occupations with which they are associated in 4th century Calleva.

Although we should be cautious in assuming that common trades like building, carpentry, leather working, textile making, brewing, fuel supply, etc, which are hard to demonstrate in the archaeological record, were established in the town through the 4th century, this is very likely to have been the case. After all, new buildings were constructed, the population required clothing and footwear, travellers looked for their stomachs to be filled and their thirst to be quenched and so on. But what is impossible to estimate are the numbers: how many carpenters, how many blacksmiths, how many masons, etc.

One activity which can be firmly evidenced involved the intensive processing of animal carcasses, a valuable raw material from which a wide range of products could be obtained. Candles of tallow (rendered animal fat) can be inferred from candle-holders, which, rather than oil lamps, were used for lighting in the late Roman town (Fig. 8.4). The marrow was not only nutritious but could also be used for high quality products such as cosmetics, soap and medicine. First noted on Insula IX in the late 2nd and 3rd centuries (Chapter 5), this processing was an extremely noisome activity which, from the state of cattle limb bones from late Roman deposits across the town, was carried out in many households, the stink carrying across the town, rather than in one industrial complex. This activity was by no means exclusive to Silchester. It has been recognised in several other towns in Britain and on the continent.

Although this activity may have mainly served local needs, some of the products may have been sold and exported from the town, which can be shown to have been well integrated into regional trade and supply networks in the 4th century (Fig. 8.8, below). One of our best sources for demonstrating these is pottery. Unlike in the 1st and early 2nd centuries when the town's needs for kitchen and storage ware were served in part by very local production, in the 4th century the nearest source were the potteries, 15 miles (24 km) distant, in the Alice Holt Forest in north-east Hampshire. These kilns had already become a significant supplier to Silchester by the 2nd century and they continued to provide half of the town's needs for kitchen and storage ware pottery through the 4th. Indeed, Alice Holt had become a major industry supplying a wide range of consumers across south-east Britain, including London.

For more specialist types of pottery like the mortaria of white clay used in the preparation of food, the town looked mainly to potteries situated to the north of the town between Dorchester-on-Thames and Oxford. This Oxfordshire industry also produced the fine, red-slipped tableware, much

FIGURE 8.4 Copper-alloy candle-stick

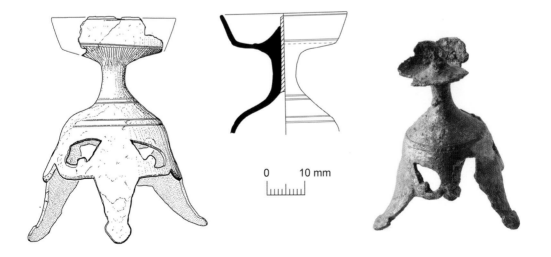

0    10 mm

0                                    100 mm

0                        50 mm

*Left:* FIGURE 8.5
Small 4th century
flagon, probably made
in the New Forest

*Right:* FIGURE 8.6
Fourth century beaker
made in the New Forest

*Below:* FIGURE 8.7
Fourth century cooking
pot made around Poole
Harbour, Dorset

0                                    100 mm

of it in forms which had been developed by the continental producers of samian ware in the 2nd century, and its products were widely consumed across the town. As well as making a similar range of red tableware, potteries in the New Forest also produced very distinctive drinking vessels with a high-fired, purple gloss finish, which were popular in Silchester and across central southern England (Figs 8.5–8.6). From even further afield came a distinctive class of cooking wares known as Black Burnished Ware made in simple clamps around Poole Harbour 70 miles (113 km) distant in south-east Dorset (Fig. 8.7). This ware, too, had begun to appear in the town in the 2nd century but was more popular in the 4th. Other British sources supplying small quantities of pottery to the town in the 4th century include the Nene Valley and Mancetter-Hartshill industries in the Midlands, the one near Peterborough, the other near Wroxeter. By this time, as we have seen with the amphorae, imports of other types of pottery, particularly the tableware and drinking vessels so evident in the 1st and 2nd centuries, are the exception. For example, the occasional sherd is noted of tableware from the Argonne region of northern France or from near Poitiers in western France.

## Transport and economy

The vitality of the networks responsible for bringing the pottery into the town from disparate sources is further demonstrated by the occurrence in the town in some quantity of stone roofing tiles which were sourced from quarries of which those in the west, in the Forest of Dean, and those to the north, in Oxfordshire at Stonesfield are the most important (Fig. 8.8). Like the pottery, these heavy tiles were carted into the town. The pale coloured limestone tiles from Stonesfield, and the dark red–maroon in the case of the Old Red Sandstone tiles from the west, came to replace the familiar red ceramic tiles of the early Roman period and would have given the town a distinctive new look.

Located at the hub of several major roads Silchester was well placed, perhaps second only to London in this regard, to receive goods from all directions and this is well reflected in their various origins. While London was probably the nearest source of most of the imported goods which reached Silchester in the early Roman period, there is little material evidence to substantiate the use of the London–Silchester road in the 4th century. Yet, in terms of strategic communication between London and the west of

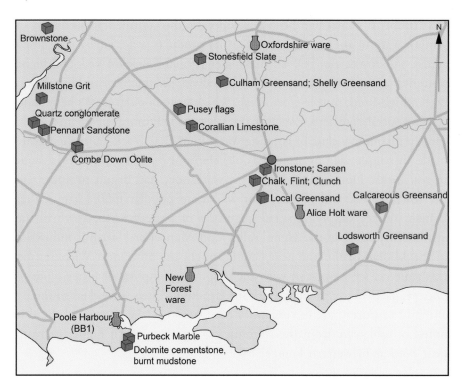

FIGURE 8.8 Map of the sources of pottery and stone found in 4th century Calleva

Britain, this section of road must have been intensively used by officials, merchants or soldiers moving between garrisons, and probably more so than any other road leading to and from Calleva. In this sense what survives in the archaeological record is not giving us a balanced picture of the differing importance and vitality of the different roads.

Supporting the movement through the town of people, horses and vehicles, whether fast two-wheeled chariots or heavy wagons pulled by oxen, must surely have remained the most important source of income for the majority of its inhabitants. As suggested above in relation to the processing of animal bone, there would also have been small-scale manufacturing of a whole variety of household and personal goods but, so far, none was so distinctive that it has been recognised both in quantity in the town and dispersed in settlements beyond. Ownership of hostelries, bars, food outlets, shops-cum-workshops, etc may have also been the principal source of income for the owners of some of the larger houses, but the likelihood is that income from their estates in the countryside supported the majority of the larger, well-endowed town houses.

Testimony to the vitality of the town are the large numbers of coins which were lost, particularly in the 50 year period between about 330 and

380, when the demand for coin stimulated mass copying. Perhaps because an individual 4th century copper alloy coin was of little intrinsic value and its loss therefore of no great consequence, thousands were lost and have subsequently been recovered by antiquarian and modern excavations across the town. Indeed, the copper nummus is the commonest non-ferrous metal find from the 4th century town.

All this economic activity would have required the keeping of accounts and records and finds of styli for writing on wax tablets remain a distinct feature of the material culture of the late Roman town. Literacy in Latin must have been prevalent among the major households as well as those engaged in some form of business, as we see with finds of styli even among the poorer households of Insula IX in the 4th century. Beyond names or numbers scratched on pottery, written records have not so far been recovered from the town. Yet there remains the promise of the scarcely explored waterlogged deposits in the south-east quarter; perhaps Silchester will eventually yield a cache of writing tablets to match the richly informative collection from the military fort of Vindolanda on the northern frontier.

While we can learn a great deal about economic life and how the population fed itself, the archaeological record is not so good at discovering how the inhabitants passed the time when they were not working. There are a few examples of bone dice and counters of bone, glass, pottery and stone which attest some playing of board games in late Roman Calleva. While these might have usually been a daytime activity, lighting by candle could supplement whatever illumination might have been given off by household fires for gaming to have been an evening or night-time activity as well.

## Dogs and cats

There is plentiful evidence for the importance of dogs and, to a lesser extent, cats in the daily life of the inhabitants in Insula IX. There are remains of dog from most of the larger groups of rubbish pits but to what extent they were regarded as pets rather than working animals is debatable. We can consider this by looking at a particular concentration in the group of rubbish and cess pits associated with the cottage in the south-east corner of the excavated area. The animals were of varying sizes and ages, including at least one neonate, with as many as at least five from one pit, four from another and perhaps as many as 11 from the pit group as a whole. They included a large adult of modern Labrador size and several small dogs, similar to terriers. The former, like the other larger animals, could have acted as a guard dog, the latter could be considered as ratters perhaps, rather than lap dogs. Study of their remains has shown that some had lived very hard lives. One elderly animal had survived a severe blow to its head, a broken rib and had substantial dental pathology before it was killed by a single blow to the head with a sharp blade. Another mature dog had also survived a severe blow to the head, the healed wound indicating subsequent osteomyelitis infection. Injuries to other animals include one with evidence of a blow across the back, another with a fracture of the left humerus which had partially united before its death, but with evidence of infection. We shall never know how these dogs came to be injured, perhaps some while they were acting to defend their owner, but, overall, the picture suggests quite an aggressive environment towards them. However, on a more positive note, another animal, less than 20 weeks old, had a healed fracture of a leg. In this case the minimal distortion and absence of evidence for infection suggests the paw was immobilised by human intervention and kept clean while healing took place.

One other dog from Insula IX deserves particular comment. It was a complete skeleton of a mature female of modern labrador size, but with jaws more characteristic of an English Bull Terrier or Rotweiller. Remarkably and uniquely it was buried, along with the remains of at least two other dogs, in a standing position in a pit in the backyard of the small building next to the cottage in the south-east of the excavated area (Fig. 8.9). There are plentiful signs of trauma: infected injury to the spine from blows to its back; multiple trauma to its left foreleg, including evidence of infection of one healing wound, such that it would have been lame at the time of death; two traumatic events visible in the skull: first, a healed depressed fracture of the muzzle caused by a substantial blow which realigned the nasal bones downwards, second, a further blow to the muzzle which had begun to heal. Although this blow was probably not sufficient to kill the dog, it died shortly afterwards. There was clearly something special about this dog for it to be buried in the way it was, not simply in a standing position, but arranged as if it was alive and, even more remarkably, in a symbolic urination stance, its right leg cocked against the side of the pit!

We shall never know the circumstances in which the injuries to these dogs were inflicted, whether by owners in moments of anger and frustration, or by villains seeking to enter the properties in question by beating off the guard dogs. Nor, until the late Roman cemeteries are excavated and the pathologies of the skeletal remains studied, will we know whether the

FIGURE 8.9 Burial in a standing position of a mature female dog in 4th century Insula IX

violence shown towards the dogs is also evident among members of the human population.

Cats are also prominent among the faunal remains in the group of pits behind the cottage in the south-east corner of Insula IX. Like the terrier-sized dogs their role was probably mainly to catch vermin but they may also have been valued for their pelts. Although there is no record of a complete skeleton in Insula IX, the burial of a complete cat was found in the rampart by the North Gate. That the grave was carefully lined with ceramic tile to create a cist suggests that this animal was a treasured pet, one which presumably belonged to the adjacent town house in Insula XXIV. Although we have seen the remarkable burial of one dog in Insula IX, it, like the other dog remains, was buried in a pit which was otherwise filled with domestic rubbish generated by a relatively poor artisanal household. The cat, on the other hand, was associated with a wealthy household and was carefully buried, insulated by the tile from its immediate environment of dumped rubbish.

# Ritual practices

The ritual, or lack of it associated with the disposal of dogs and cats leads us to consider what we have learned of other ritual practices in late Roman Calleva. In the first place we must note that the rubbish and cess pits which contained the remains of dogs (and cats) also contained the remains of human neonates, also with a cluster in the pit group at the back of the cottage in the south-east of the excavated area of Insula IX. Among what might originally have been four individuals, only one was represented by an almost complete skeleton. Although a few were premature or stillborn, the majority had reached full-term. Why these infants were disposed of in the same way as dogs, cats and household rubbish in general when they could have been formally buried in a cemetery outside the walls is completely unclear. Although we do not yet have an excavated late Roman cemetery at Silchester, the one at Poundbury outside the town of Dorchester, Dorset contained infant burials. However, excavation within that town has also shown that, at the same time, infant remains were being disposed of in rubbish and cess pits along with those of dogs and cats just like in Silchester. We can only conjecture the reasons for this behaviour, but it represents the continuation of a broader tradition of infant burial either within or close to buildings within the town that began soon after the Roman conquest and was allowed by Roman law.

Other practices which have been documented in late Roman Silchester and which are difficult to explain include the burial of complete pottery vessels in pits which do not seem to have been dug for the primary purpose of general rubbish disposal and were located some distance from the houses. This is in addition to previously recognised behaviour, which goes back to the late Iron Age occupation at Calleva, where complete or near-complete pots were deposited at the bottom of wells and, as in previous centuries, some deliberately pierced in the belly. Several instances of such pits were recorded in Insula IX, a few with little or no other associated finds, but one with some cattle bone and fragments of drinking vessels. This kind of association of animal bone and significant quantities of pottery drinking vessels is typical of a second group of pits in Insula IX where the pottery is dominated by fragments of such vessels. These might readily be explained as the remains of celebrations involving feasting and drinking. Pits with these kinds of contents were also among those located at a distance from the houses.

The contents of the pits and wells have given us valuable insight into the daily life of the inhabitants, the food they ate, their occupations, the occasional celebration which needed to be marked by special deposits of the resulting waste, and also particular circumstances which precipitated the disposal of infants, cats and dogs along with other rubbish next to the buildings with which they were associated. Since these latter acts filled up and therefore closed the use of the cess pit in question, they might be connected with a major event in the household, such as the loss of a baby or, perhaps, the death or departure of members of the household, even leading to a complete change of the occupants. We shall return to the subject of pits and wells with distinctive types of find in the next chapter as they are also an important feature of the latest occupation within Insula IX and its eventual abandonment.

# CHAPTER NINE

# The end

..............................................................................................................

Calleva is one of only of a handful of the major towns of Roman Britain which did not re-emerge in the late Saxon period and then become a major town of England or Wales. Its situation most closely resembles that of the tribal capitals of Venta Icenorum (Caistor-by-Norwich) in Norfolk and Viroconium (Wroxeter) in Shropshire where the Roman towns are now almost completely devoid of buildings. In both cases, as at Silchester, the medieval parish church is located just inside the Roman defences. Farm buildings also survive at Silchester and Wroxeter: at the former next to the church, now gentrified as the Old Manor House, and more centrally at Wroxeter, next to the modern museum set within the Roman town. Other major towns like Venta Silurum (Caerwent) in Gwent and Isurium Brigantum (Aldborough) in Yorkshire are now villages rather than towns, their churches at the centre of what was the Roman town. Verulamium is similarly partly open, its church on the site of the forum basilica, but modern St Albans presses close against the Roman town, the abbey founded on what was believed to be the site of Alban's martyrdom in the early 3rd century. The aim of this chapter is to explore how Calleva came to be the greenfield site it is today.

Roman control of Britain ceased in 409 and the towns with their administrative districts were on their own. Units of the army had already been withdrawn to tackle dangerous issues across the Channel in Gaul and by 409 there may have only been skeleton garrisons on Hadrian's Wall and in other forts in the north, in Wales and around the coast which were still occupied at the beginning of the 5th century. Calleva, like other towns across Britain, was well protected by its massive city wall, but that was only effective as long as there was manpower to police it and the inhabitants within. In such circumstances the town would have been an attractive haven in a time of insecurity for those living in unprotected farms in the countryside.

There can be little doubt that life changed dramatically for the great majority of the population of Britain at the beginning of the 5th century. Without an army to support and without an administration to purchase supplies for it and to organise the collection of taxes, the economic life of the towns would have sharply declined. To illustrate this, almost no new Roman gold and silver coin entered the province after 407, the supply of bronze coin having stopped in 402. A sign of stress in the silver currency can be seen in the way that the weight of the individual coins was reduced by systematically clipping silver off around their circumference. The consequences of the abandonment of Britain would have piled one on another: the loss of demand for staple foodstuffs to feed the army and the administration would have immediately affected not only estate owners but also the merchants and those responsible for carting harvests to wherever they were required. If the army had been withdrawn, leaving only skeletal garrisons, there would have been a consequential loss of troop movements. All this would have had a serious impact on a town like Calleva whose vitality so much depended on the traffic which passed through it. How, for example, did all those businesses located along the principal streets of the town manage with much reduced activity?

With little prospect of a return to Roman control, those with the portable wealth to take with them and start a new life elsewhere could leave their estates and Britain altogether and head south across the Channel to Gaul. The great late Roman treasure hoards like those from Hoxne, Mildenhall, Thetford and Water Newton in the east of England show that some had indeed accumulated vast wealth with the capacity to move elsewhere. Indeed, there is a record of Britons settling in Brittany in the 5th century. For Calleva, this might mean that some of the larger town houses were abandoned early in the 5th century, but not necessarily before. After Cirencester, with seven or eight finds of gold coins dating between 364 and 402, Silchester has six such finds. The eventual loss of wealthy households would have impacted not only on the economy of the town but also on its administration. Would any kind of centralised authority have survived for very long in the town after 409?

How do these scenarios relate to what we have learned of life in the town at the beginning of the 5th century? First, as a general indicator of economic activity, excavations within the town have consistently produced examples of the latest copper coins to have been brought into Britain up to 402.

Although the coins of the last emperors – Theodosius I, Honorius, Arcadius and Eugenius – retaining control over Britain are not as abundant as issues earlier in the 4th century, they are found across the town: widely across the excavated areas of Insulas III and IX, in the basilica (of the forum basilica) and in the baths. If the concentration of coins found at the north end of the great basilica relate to taxation or any other kind of official business, it is notable that it includes two examples of silver siliquas, one of which, dated 388–392, is of Theodosius I. Although the antiquarians found a very few other examples of these silver coins, there are no others from modern excavations, illustrating just how rare they are as casual losses. The finds from the forum basilica not only re-inforce the idea that their loss was related to some exceptional, probably official activity, but that this was certainly going on in the closing years of the 4th, if not into the 5th century. The coins from elsewhere across the town indicate continuity of activity through the later 4th into the beginning of the 5th century. Importantly, economic activity as revealed by coin loss is no different at Silchester than at other towns in central southern Britain, but how long business using coin continued after the rupture of 409 is, in the light of the scenario sketched out above, debatable, but may not have extended much if at all beyond 410. Barter (in which coin singly or in bulk, as a copper alloy commodity, could have played a part) is likely to have increasingly become the norm in the years after 409.

Another sign of life continuing at or near normal at the very end of the 4th or beginning of the 5th comes from the public baths where a new heated room was built sometime after 388 (Fig. 8.1). We cannot say exactly when this happened and, depending when the coin was lost, it may have been early in the 5th century, but it signifies how important it was to maintain the public baths, or at least a part of them. Some remarkable finds show that the baths were being used by men and women of wealth and status into the 5th century (Figs 9.1–9.2). Although we can see with hindsight that such a re-furbishment project of a public building was undertaken close to the withdrawal of the Roman administration, for the inhabitants of Calleva there was no reason to suppose an imminent crisis, let alone one different in scale to those which had beset the province earlier. Indeed there may have been considerable optimism in those opening years of the 5th century when the British usurper emperor, Constantine III, took a field army, with presumably the resources to sustain it, across the Channel to try and regain control of northern Gaul and Germany from the barbarian tribes who crossed the Rhine in large numbers in the winter of 406–7. Britain seemed a relatively secure springboard from which such adventures could be launched.

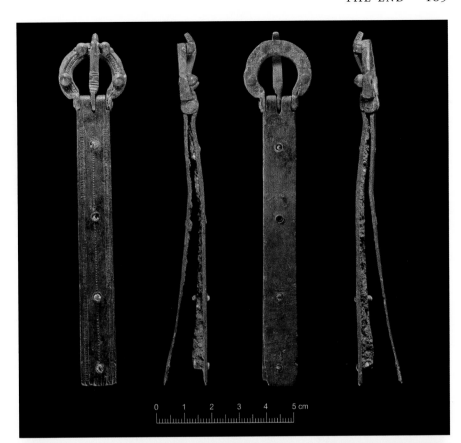

FIGURE 9.1 Late 4th/
early 5th century copper
alloy belt fitting of a
Roman official found
beside the public baths
(PHOTO BY IAN R. CARTWRIGHT)

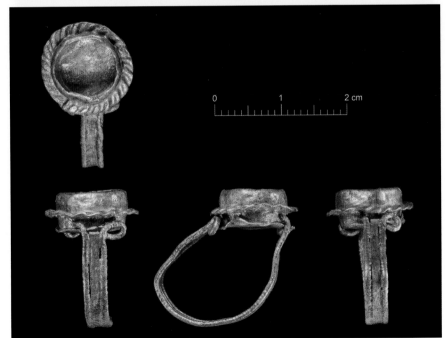

FIGURE 9.2 Late
Roman gold finger ring
lost at the site of the
public baths
(PHOTO BY IAN R. CARTWRIGHT)

But then, what must surely have seemed like a catastrophe happened and very different circumstances prevailed in Calleva, as they did across Roman Britain as a whole. The conditions for supporting town life had been withdrawn and between 409 and probably no later than the mid-7th century the settlement was either completely or almost completely abandoned and the vacated land gradually given over to agriculture. There are no artefacts from the town which can be dated with any confidence to between the 6th or 7th century and the 10th or 11th century. However, we know that by the time of Domesday (1086) there was certainly a small community at Silchester and that the settlement was concentrated at the eastern end of the walled town and focused on the church of St Mary the Virgin, which was built just inside the town wall in the late 11th or 12th century. Where did they live before that? Although material culture of the 'missing' centuries between Roman and medieval is rare, it is quite possible that evidence will eventually emerge, as it has in other places in Britain, to show a degree of continuity of occupation. Is it, for example, a coincidence that St Mary's lies close to a late Roman inhumation cemetery in which it is probable that Christians were buried? The cemetery is located immediately adjacent, outside the town wall to the east.

There are now several strands of evidence to show how the community responded to the events of the early 5th century. One of these relates to the security – or insecurity – of the community; another to the question of continuing life within the town after the beginning of the century, a third to the story of the final abandonment of properties and, finally, a slender strand which considers what might have happened to the town during the rise of the Anglo-Saxon kingdoms of Mercia and Wessex.

## Increasing insecurity

The community was well protected by its massive town wall, but obviously vulnerable to attack at the gates and three have good evidence of complete or partial blocking, but with no indication when this might have happened. First, the south-east postern gate, which seems to have provided a link between the mansio and an unexcavated building just outside the wall, was completely blocked by mortared courses of flint and ceramic roofing-tile (Fig. 9.3). This could well have happened before 409, but almost certainly not much later when it would have become clear that the services of the mansio were no longer required. Similar good quality work, also perhaps

FIGURE 9.3 Blocking of the south-east postern gate, view from inside the town

hinting at a relatively early date, reduced the South-west Gate to a width of only 2 m. Third, the West Gate, where the south carriageway was blocked, again, at an unknown date, but after the demolition of the forum basilica as it contained a fragment of one of its Corinthian capitals as well as a section of double column. When the forum basilica might have been demolished will be explored further below, but it is likely to have been long after the beginning of the 5th century. The blocking of the West Gate, then, was not necessarily prompted by the reduction in road traffic which would have surely followed soon after the break with Rome. Whether it was matched by a similar blocking at the poorly preserved East Gate is not known, but likely. The situation at the North and South gates is equally uncertain: columnar material, also probably originally from the forum basilica but not built in to create a structure recognisable as a blocking of the carriageways, is illustrated by Joyce in his diary. If the structure attached to the inside face of the town wall, identified by geophysics within the churchyard, is indeed as it would seem, a gate, it too was blocked at an unknown date.

   This attention to the gates of the town suggests a continuation of some authority after 409, one that was capable of organising guards to monitor incoming traffic. The possibility of a larger defence force is hinted at by the discovery in 1991 of a skull radiocarbon dated to the 5th century in the town wall ditch outside the North Gate. Was this a victim of an attack whose head was displayed above the gate as a deterrent? Interestingly, another skull was found close by in the antiquarian excavation of 1909. Given that the areas explored by both 20th century excavations outside the North Gate were limited in extent, the intriguing possibility remains of more extensive finds of human remains in the ditch.

The insecurity of the time at the beginning of the 5th century is well brought out by the discovery in the 1980s of a small hoard of three complete gold finger-rings, fragments of a fourth, one fragmentary silver ring and 56 silver coins (Figs 9.4–9.5). It had been buried, presumably by someone leaving rather than on the point of entering the town, around the fateful year of 409/10 just outside the town wall between the West and South-west gates. The size of the collection suggest it was an individual's store of wealth but we can only speculate on the circumstances of its concealment. Perhaps it had been stolen, the thief hurriedly burying it to escape his pursuers? Two other hoards, whose contents of iron artefacts have already been introduced in Chapter 8, were concealed, certainly no earlier than the 4th century

FIGURE 9.4 Two gold finger rings from a small hoard of gold and silver jewellery and coins, including 56 silver siliquae, found just outside the town wall near the West Gate

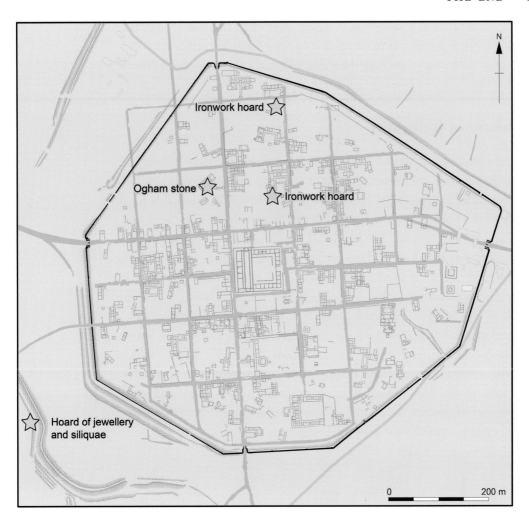

and quite possibly much later, in deep pits, possibly abandoned wells (Fig. 9.5). One was close to one of the two town houses in Insula I, the other close to the street bordering the east side of Insula XXIII and a few metres north of one of the two town houses in that block. Both hoards contained a great mix of artefacts (see Fig. 8.3): were these objects collected by the households besides which they were buried and perhaps gathered from both their country estate and their town house? The miscellaneous character of the two hoards suggests that the constituent items were not in regular use but were nevertheless perceived to have value and worth storing away, their concealment perhaps prompted by their owners either leaving Calleva and unable to take all the contents of their houses with them or choosing to reduce their store of tools and equipment down to what was in regular, daily use. We simply cannot know what precisely motivated the burying of these collections, but it is difficult to imagine it happening at any other time than one of great uncertainty such as the years following the break with Rome.

## The house of Tebicatos

The recent excavations of Insula IX probably give us the best insight into how life might have continued after the beginning of the 5th century. This project was able to explore the context of one of the most remarkable finds, and one of the latest, from the Roman town, discovered during the Society of Antiquaries' excavations. This is a dwarf Roman column, complete except for its capital, which is inscribed in ogham, that is the language is Irish Celtic but the letters are from the Latin alphabet (Fig. 9.6). These were formed by scoring horizontal or oblique strokes either side of a vertical axis: for example B L V S N are denoted by one, two, three, four and five strokes at right-angles and on the right of the axis; H D T C Q by one to five strokes similarly, on the left, and so on. The text reads TEBICATO[S] / [MAQ]I MUCO[I..] which can be translated as (The something) of Tebicatos, son of the tribe of (?). The missing word at the beginning is usually taken to be 'memorial' or 'stone', but 'land' is also possible, given that, in an Irish context, ogham inscriptions were used to denote familial title to land.

0                                      1 m

FIGURE 9.6
Left: the ogham stone as found in Insula IX in 1893; right: drawing showing the ogham inscription and the profile of the damaged Roman dwarf column

The stone was found, point downwards, during the Antiquaries' exploration of Insula IX in 1893 at the bottom of a well dug some 2.7 m below the Roman ground surface (Fig. 9.5). Beneath the stone and partly flattened by it was a pewter flagon whose belly had been deliberately pierced (Fig. 9.7). The recent excavation of Insula IX has clarified the context of the find: the well is situated in the backyard of the small cottage in the south-east corner of the excavated area (Fig. 9.8). What remains at issue is the date of the ogham inscription and the date when the stone was buried, bearing in mind that its deposition effectively ended the use of the well. The latter presumably coinciding with the final abandonment of the cottage. More intriguing is to explore the reasons why an Irishman was in Silchester at this time and why he thought to advertise his presence so overtly. How many of the inhabitants of the town could read ogham?

Ogham was an Irish invention with many examples of inscribed stones from the island, particularly from southern Ireland. There are also examples of such inscribed stones from south-west Wales and from Cornwall and Devon; but the Silchester stone is the only find in England east of the River Severn. There is no certainty as to when ogham was first developed but it is generally agreed that it had happened by about 400 and that the language of the Silchester stone is consistent with an early date, perhaps in the first half of the 5th century, for the inscription. While we know where the stone ended up, we only have the shape of it as a dwarf Roman column to guide us to where it was originally located. It was probably designed to support the roof of a verandah or portico such as the one which graced the north-facing 'front' elevation of the adjacent cottage (see Figs 7.10, 8.2). Although this modest house does not otherwise seem to merit such architectural adornment, it is hard to explain why the stone ended up in the well in its backyard unless it was originally part of the verandah. A coin of Theodosius I from a pit within one of the tower rooms indicates the building was still complete at the beginning of the 5th century. How long it remained standing is unknown, but a subsequent pit which cut through the foundations of one of the tower rooms suggests partial demolition perhaps later in the 5th century, the core of the house remaining standing. We can only guess when the remainder of the building was demolished – perhaps sometime in the 6th century?

FIGURE 9.7
The pierced and dented pewter flagon crushed by the ogham stone

Piercing

0                              250 mm

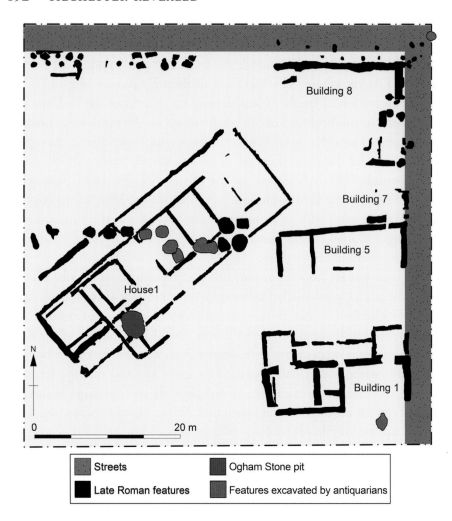

FIGURE 9.8 The context of the Ogham stone in late Roman Insula IX

With this ogham inscription we have for the first time the identity of the owner or occupant of a Callevan house of any period. If an early 5th century date is correct for the date of the ogham, Tebicatus was in residence by then. Interestingly the latest find from the group of cess and rubbish pits at the back of the cottage is a decorated copper alloy armlet dated to the late 4th or early 5th century. As has been suggested in the previous chapter, the character of the finds, which include the remains of neonates, cats and dogs, from some of these pits may be consistent with clearance following a major event in the household, such as a death or the complete abandonment of the property.

Such an abandonment at the end of the 5th/beginning of the 5th century would have provided the opportunity for occupation of the house by Tebicatus, alone or with an accompanying household. It is then that he could have made the inscription, announcing his ownership of the property. How old he was when he arrived in Calleva is, of course, unknown, but he was probably in his late teens or early 20s and he may then have lived for another 20 or 30 years which would take his death to around the mid-5th century. As there was no sign of a body in or near the well where the ogham stone was placed, the burial of the stone may have merely marked the departure, rather than the demise of Tebicatus, one which involved the removal of the column and demolition of at least the verandah, if not the whole of the north-facing elevation of the building. On balance, Tebicatus's time in Calleva was probably confined within the first half of the 5th century, but we do have to be open to the possibility of a later chronology since the MAQI MUCOI formula was used throughout the life of the ogham script. We cannot exclude a 6th or early 7th century date.

We are still left with the puzzle why an Irishman was in Calleva at all. Knowledge of ogham suggests he was learned, perhaps a leading member of a southern Irish tribe. And, although the carving of the inscription may have been simply the execution of an established custom on taking possession of a new property, it does raise the possibility that there were other Irish in the town at the same time capable of reading and writing ogham. V-profiled grooves on the other side of the stone from the inscription suggest the sharpening of a weapon point. Was he perhaps a member of a group of mercenaries who had been hired to defend Calleva after the break with Rome? Silchester was, of course, on the main road from south Wales to London, a route likely to be taken by Christian pilgrims following the conversion by St Patrick on their way to Rome and who wished to avoid the longer and more dangerous sea-crossing from southern Ireland across the Bay of Biscay to the west coast of France. Was Tebicatus himself a pilgrim? Even if the questions raised by its discovery outnumber the possible answers, the Silchester ogham stone gives a fascinating insight into the history of Calleva following the break with Rome.

The burial of the ogham stone was also an effective decommissioning of the well with no evidence of a successor or of any later occupation in the vicinity. Similar evidence for their deliberate infilling was found in the other wells in the excavated part of Insula IX. One contained a deposit of cattle bone, including burnt bone, another an unusual number of a particular type of artefact, in this case toilet instruments, suggesting deliberate choice in what was placed in it. This naturally takes us on to consider what circumstances might have occasioned abandonment of the settlement and the associated decommissioning of wells.

# Where did all the people go?

At some time between the 5th and, probably, the 7th century the area within the walls was devoid of settlement with just the possibility that it had shrunk to a small nucleus on and outside the town wall on the eastern side. Was this a gradual process, or, as the deliberate infilling of wells in Insula IX suggests, was it accelerated for some reason at a particular point in time? What might have occasioned the demolition and removal of buildings from the interior of the town?

To gain some understanding of what might have occurred we need to return to the forum basilica and explore what might have happened to this building after the break with Rome. We saw earlier that the coins of the House of Theodosius show that the basilica certainly continued in use into at least the early 5th century, but how much longer after that? In addition to a fragment of glass with engraved decoration which is thought to be post-Roman, there are pieces of blue-green window glass with streaks of red running through them which are typical of early Anglo-Saxon ecclesiastical sites in the north of England. Although we do not have to conclude that the presence of such glass necessarily equates with an ecclesiastical interpretation, it is tempting to do so and it potentially lengthens the occupation of the basilica to the 7th century. Whether or not the building by the south-east corner of the forum basilica was a church, it has no evidence of occupation beyond the mid-4th century. Moreover, the massively constructed forum basilica offered a much more secure location for worship. A monastic community might help explain why, when the interior of the town is completely devoid of any trace of a Roman building, the entire circuit of the town wall survives to this day and in places to a considerable height. If the search for suitable building material was a motive for robbing stone from the abandoned town, then taking it from the nearest source, the town wall, was an obvious choice. However, if there was still an authority, such as a monastery, in control of what was left of the town, priority might well have been given to clearing the interior to create the sacred precinct protected by the town wall as the vallum monasterii, the rampart of the monastery. This would have provided the context for the final abandonment of houses and the deliberate infilling of their wells.

This is highly speculative but, in the context of the febrile politics of early Anglo-Saxon England when Silchester lay on the boundary between the kingdoms of Wessex and Mercia, the neutralisation of the town by creating a monastic community at its heart might have been welcomed by both parties. Most of the buildings within the town were probably of timber-frame construction on mortared flint or gravel foundations and so easily taken down and the timbers recycled or used as fuel. This left the earlier largely or wholly masonry buildings such as the forum basilica, the baths and, probably, the mansio (and its baths). While some of these structures were demolished to ground level, the west range of the forum basilica and part of the baths were much more deeply robbed, perhaps at a later time when building materials had become scarce and the foundations of other walls previously taken down had become invisible (Fig. 9.9). When either stage of demolition took place is unknown, but it was probably not until the late Saxon period when local church building required materials that the first stage (to ground level) happened. Later phases of church building, including that of St Mary the Virgin at Silchester itself, might have seen the removal of the remainder of the Roman masonry within the town walls which were left to serve as a boundary to the fields within the town.

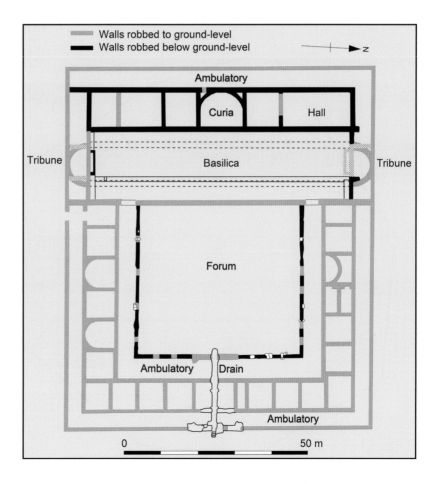

FIGURE 9.9 The different phases of the robbing of stone from the forum basilica; the more deeply robbed range of rooms alongside the west side of the basilica perhaps standing much later than the rest of the building

# Medieval Silchester

By the time of Domesday in the late 11th century Silchester was a small community centred on the church of St Mary, just inside the town walls, but spreading north to the amphitheatre and south along the outside of the town wall towards the South Gate (Fig. 9.10). The defensive potential of the earthworks which formed the amphitheatre was realised in the 12th century when there is evidence for the construction of a palisade around the crest of the bank and a re-furbishment of the entrances (Fig. 9.11). Within the defended enclosure was a post-built timber hall and subsidiary buildings, an occupancy which may well have coincided with the civil war between King Stephen (1135–1154) and Matilda. The village probably shrank down to a few buildings close to the church and the amphitheatre in the second half of the 14th century, perhaps following the Black Death of 1347. The

FIGURE 9.10 Outline plan of medieval Silchester

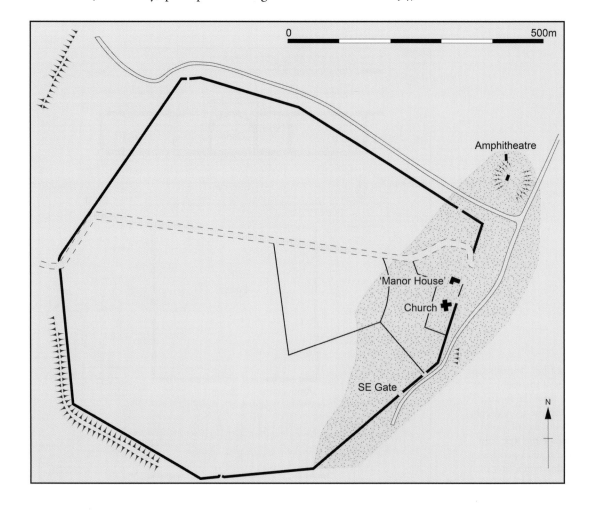

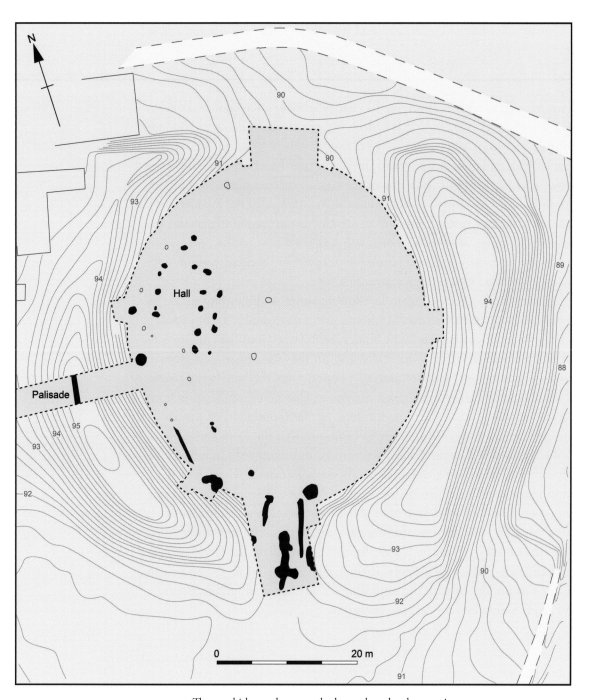

FIGURE 9.II The amphitheatre between the late IIth and I3th centuries

oldest and only surviving houses of the residual village are the cottage on the north side of the amphitheatre and what is now the Old Manor House next to the church.

Why no revival? Why did Silchester's subsequent history diverge from that of the great majority of the major Roman towns of Britain? Why did it not emerge as a town again like its near neighbours, Chichester, London and Winchester? Although it has been suggested that Silchester did not flourish because it was not on a river, this was clearly not an issue at the time of its foundation at the end of the 1st century BC. In the late Iron Age it was a far-reaching entrepôt, one of the best connected places in southern Britain. During the Roman occupation the importance of the road network ensured a vibrant history right up to its end at the beginning of the 5th century. Wroxeter, we should remember, was sited next to the Severn, but proximity to that river did not ensure its recovery in late Saxon times and, like Silchester, it, too, became a greenfield site.

As long as the road west from London remained an important means of communication, then Calleva's future was assured. However, at some point, perhaps when Silchester was in the border territory between the kingdoms of Wessex and Mercia, its fate was sealed and, in the fragmented post-Roman world, the east–west road connecting London with the west was broken. With important early Anglo-Saxon activity at Dorchester-on-Thames from the late 4th/early 5th century, re-inforced by the foundation of the abbey and the appointment of Birinus as its bishop in 635, the focus shifted back to the Thames. Wallingford was chosen to be one of Alfred's burghs in the 9th century and Reading was already of some significance when the Viking army chose to camp there in the winter of 870–1, becoming even more important with the foundation of its abbey by Henry I in 1121. Further down the river, Old Windsor was the site of a royal palace in the 9th century, later superseded by Windsor Castle, founded by William the Conqueror in the later 11th century. The River Thames and control of its crossings had become all important with the unification of the Saxon kingdoms to create the English kingdom in the 10th century.

# Postscript

Even after almost 50 years of new investigations, and a little over 150 years since the start of excavations by that pioneer archaeologist, the Reverend Joyce, it must be apparent that we are still only at the beginning of our exploration of the archaeology of Iron Age and Roman Calleva. While some of the recent work has, by modern standards and expectations, been on a large scale, the total area that has been explored since 1974 amounts to between only 1% and 2% of the surface area within the city walls; and almost no work has been done on the suburbs and cemeteries outside them. Nevertheless, the published new information arising from these excavations and surveys is much more wide-ranging and detailed in scope than all the reports generated by the work of Joyce and the Society of Antiquaries. Looking to the future it is perfectly reasonable to imagine a continuing increase in the amount of new knowledge that could, potentially, be generated from each square or cubic metre of a new excavation – less really would mean more.

The possible scope of new projects seems almost infinite, whether it might involve working on public buildings, like the mansio, the temples, or the forum next the basilica; private housing; the shops and workshops lining the main east–west street of the city, or the people buried in the cemeteries outside the city, and so on. And, just as new questions and new methodologies emerge, fresh research will be carried out on the finds and environmental evidence which have already been made and archived.

We should remember, too, that, while past research focused first on the Roman city, then the Iron Age and the Roman city, we also need to be aware that there are traces of an earlier prehistoric settlement about which we know virtually nothing. Is this evidence of casual settlement, or is there a much deeper history to the Silchester promontory which was a factor in drawing the late Iron Age settlers to this particular location, rather than elsewhere in the neighbourhood? Was Calleva where Commius settled around 50 BC? On the other hand, and coming closer to the present, there is still much to learn about the medieval village which clustered around the church of St Mary the Virgin and what happened in the 500 years or so between the end of the Roman city and the first visible signs of the medieval village in the 10th/11th century.

More important, still, is the need to continue to conserve this unique Iron Age and Roman city of Calleva in perpetuity. Midway between busy Basingstoke and Reading, ancient Silchester is a peaceful and beautiful space. Conservation from as recent as the 1990s has not weathered well, vegetation springing back along the walls, while the amphitheatre is neglected and in urgent need of attention. While it is vital for the remains of the Roman city to retain its undeveloped and unchanging rural character, the steady flow of visitors, day after day, needs to be carefully managed. The authorities charged with looking after the site can surely do better than a pot-holed car park, a portable toilet and a few information panels. As for future presentation and interpretation, this is the age to exploit the opportunities that the rapid developments in digital technologies allow, whether at Silchester itself in a visitor centre, decades overdue to replace the long-closed Calleva Museum, or in the Silchester Gallery at Reading Museum.

# Further information and reading

................................................................

## Visiting Silchester

The Roman walls and amphitheatre are looked after by English Heritage and can be visited free of charge at any reasonable time. Allow 1–2 hours for walking a complete circuit of the walls and visiting the amphitheatre.

## Museum

The Silchester Gallery in Reading Museum displays some of the outstanding finds from past excavations

## Further reading

Silchester has generated an extensive bibliography and the following guide must, necessarily, be selective.

For a short introduction to the Iron Age and Roman town, see the English Heritage Guidebook: M. Fulford, *Silchester Roman Town* (2017).

George Boon's *Silchester. The Roman Town of Calleva* (1974) brings together the results of the antiquarian excavations, particularly those of Reverend Joyce and the Society of Antiquaries, and is the starting point for deeper investigations into Silchester's archaeology before the 1970s. John Creighton and Robert Fry's *Silchester: changing visions of a Roman town* (2016) presents, through geophysical survey and a re-mapping of earlier discoveries, a new plan of the town and its immediate environs. It contains an insula by insula, area by area, summary of past findings and includes a comprehensive bibliography of publications on the Iron Age and Roman Town up to 2014.

The other principal sources which underpin this book are, for the Iron Age (Chapter 2): M. Fulford, A. Clarke, E. Durham and N. Pankhurst, *Late Iron Age Calleva: the pre-conquest occupation at Insula IX* (2018), and M. Fulford and J. Timby *Late Iron Age and Roman Silchester: excavations on the site of the forum basilica 1977, 1980–86* (2000). The latter is also relevant for all subsequent chapters. For building a picture of Calleva in the first decades after the Roman invasion of AD 43 (Chapter 3), see M. Fulford, A. Clarke, E. Durham and N. Pankhurst, *Silchester Insula IX: the Claudio-Neronian occupation of the Iron Age* oppidum (2020). M. Fulford and A. Clarke's *Silchester: city in transition* (2011) informs Chapters 4 and 5. M. Fulford, A. Clarke and H. Eckardt, *Life and Labour in Late Roman Silchester. Excavations in Insula IX since 1997* (2006) sheds light on later Roman Silchester (Chapter 7–9). For the transition from Roman town to medieval village, see M. Fulford, *Calleva Atrebatum* (Silchester, Hampshire, UK): an early medieval extinction, in N. Christie and A. Augenti (eds), *Urbes Extinctae* (2012), 331–51.

Sources for work on public buildings include M. Fulford and J. Timby on the forum basilica (cited above); for the amphitheatre: M. Fulford, *The Silchester Amphitheatre: excavations of 1979–85* (1989); and for the defences: *Silchester: excavations on the defences 1974–80* (1984) and J. R.L. Allen, *The Masonry Defences of Roman Silchester (Calleva Atrebatum), North Hampshire* (2013). Excavation of the public baths is ongoing at the time of writing.

J. Halstead's and M. Fulford's *Silchester: life on the dig* (2015) gives a colourful impression of daily life on the Insula IX excavation 1997–2014.

### Roman Britain – Silchester in context

There are many general and accessible surveys of late Iron Age and Roman Britain, eg: P. Salway, *Roman Britain: a very short introduction* (2000), G. de la Bédoyère, *Roman Britain. A New History* (2006), R. Hobbs and R. Jackson, *Roman Britain: life at the edge of empire* (2010), C. Higgins, *Under Another Sky: Journeys in Roman Britain* (2013); for the more academic, see D. Mattingly, *An Imperial Possession: Britain in the Roman Empire: 54 BC–AD 409* (2006) and, more recently, M. Millett, L. Revell and A. Moore (eds), *The Oxford Handbook of Roman Britain* (2016).

### Silchester in fiction

Silchester has inspired the writing of historical fiction, notably Rosemary Suttcliff's *The Eagle of the Ninth* (1954) (made into a film, *The Eagle* (2011)) and its sequel, *The Silver Branch* (1957), both drawing on Joyce's account of the discovery of the Silchester Eagle. Subsequently the town has been the setting for both a late Roman story: P. Vansittart, *Three Six Seven* (1983) and an early one, set around the time of the conquest: S. Scarrow, *The Eagle and the Wolves* (2003).

# Index

..................................................................................................................................